Your Best Years

Your
Best
Years

by
J. Oswald Sanders

MOODY PRESS
CHICAGO

Library of Congress Cataloging in Publication Data

Sanders, J. Oswald (John Oswald), 1902-
  Your best years.

  Includes indexes.
  1. Aged — Religious life. 2. Aged — Conduct of life. I. Title.
BV4580.S23   248.8'5   82-7846
ISBN 0-8024-0455-3   AACR2

2 3 4 5 6 7 Printing/LC/Year 87 86 85 84 83

Printed in the United States of America

Contents

5

Preface

When first the suggestion was put to me that I should write a book dealing with the problem of aging and the aged, the idea had little appeal. But on further thought, I realized that the considerable experience, both personal and vicarious, that I had had in that area might be valuable to others, and should be shared. Since I have almost attained octogenarian status, I am able to have a very real empathy with those in like case.

Life has brought me into intimate contact with many aging people, both in my own family circle and in the course of missionary administration. My wife and I had aged parents living with us for a number of years. When he was eighty, my father was struck by a streetcar and lay in our home in a coma for two years. After a period of illness my first wife died of cancer. Some time afterward I married again. My second wife contracted multiple sclerosis and was ill for more than two years before she was called home.

As director of a large and long-established missionary society, inevitably I had considerable contact with the aging problems of retired members. A preaching ministry of more than fifty years has also given me insight into both the joys and the disabilities of the aged. I desire to share both the results of my own observation and, more importantly, what I have gleaned from better qualified authorities in this field.

It is my deepening conviction that, through lack of reliable information, many elderly people are laboring under handicaps that are quite unnecessary. The pains and disabilities of senescence — both physical and psychological — are painfully real, but modern medical knowledge and treatment can make the baneful effects considerably more tolerable. In addition, the Christian has available resources that too often remain untapped.

7

It has been my aim to treat the subject in a positive manner. Without minimizing or oversimplifying the realities of the aging process, let me note that there is an optimistic and cheerful outlook on old age that does not receive sufficient emphasis. Realism and optimism with regard to the aging process can sleep in the same bed. In many cases it is possible to face the facts squarely and yet adopt an attitude — a mind-set — that will enable one to triumph over the adverse factors in old age and enjoy the many positive blessings and opportunities it can bring. May that be the case with the reader.

I have included many poems, for very often poets and hymn writers have the gift of compressing into a few vivid words important truths that can sound pedestrian and lose their impact when expressed in plain prose.

A SEVENTEENTH-CENTURY NUN'S PRAYER

LORD, Thou knowest better than I myself
  Know that I am growing older and
  Will some day be old.
Keep me from the fatal habit of thinking
  I must say something on every subject
  and on every occasion.
Release me from the craving to straighten
  out everybody's affairs.
Make me thoughtful, but not moody;
  helpful, but not bossy.
With my vast store of wisdom it seems
  a pity not to use it all, but Thou
  knowest, O Lord, that I want a
  few friends at the end.
Keep my mind free from the recital
  of endless details; give me wings to
  get to the point.
Seal my lips on my aches and pains. They are
  increasing, and love of rehearsing them is
  becoming sweeter as the days go by.
I dare not ask for grace enough to enjoy the
  tales of others' pains, but help me to
  endure them with patience.
I dare not ask for an improved memory,
  but for a growing humility and a lessening
  cocksureness when my memory seems to
  clash with the memories of others.
Teach me the glorious lesson that
  occasionally I may be mistaken.
Keep me reasonably sweet; I do not
  want to be a saint — some of them
  are so hard to live with — but a sour
  old person is one of the crowning
  works of the devil.
Give me the ability to see good things in
  unexpected places, and talents in
  unexpected people.
And give me, O Lord, the grace to tell
  them so. Amen.

1

Old Age Has Compensations

Old age is not always—or usually—equated with joy and enjoyment. Rather it is popularly viewed as an unfortunate and unhappy period of life that cannot be avoided and must therefore be accepted with the best grace possible. But that is not a biblical concept, nor is it shared by all.

"Old age, far from being an embarrassment, is in fact a golden opportunity for human growth and deep happiness," said one aging man.[1] His concept is much nearer the scriptural ideal. The Preacher contended that "a gray head is a crown of glory; it is found in the way of righteousness" (Proverbs 16:31).

There are some aging Christians who radiate joy, and whose very presence is a benediction. Like Barnabas, they are "sons of encouragement" (Acts 4:36). Are they special favorites of the Lord, or could it be that they have mastered a secret discipline and so fully opened their lives to the influence of the Holy Spirit that they are able to triumph over the inevitable limitations of age?

That was certainly the case with John Wesley. When he was an old man, this testimony was borne to the radiance of his personality: "Wherever he went he diffused a portion of his own felicity. In him old age appeared delightful, like an evening without a cloud. And it was impossible to observe him without wishing, 'May my latter end be like his!' "[2]

Although the joys of age and youth may differ in incidence and boisterousness, the one can be as attractive and infectious as the other. Enjoyment of life, even in old age, can be quite independent of present circumstances.

"I have learned to be content in whatever circumstances I am" (Philippians 4:11), testified the prematurely aged Paul. When he exhorted the Philippian Christians: "Rejoice in the Lord always;

again I will say, rejoice!'' (Philippians 4:4), he was not reclining in a rocking chair in a palace. He was chained to a soldier in a Roman prison, but that did not rob him of his contentment and joy in God.

Our Lord bequeathed His surplus of joy to His followers. ''These things I have spoken to you,'' He said, ''that My joy may be in you, and that your joy may be made full'' (John 15:11). His bequest was to the old as well as to the young, for in Christ there is neither young nor old.

The joy of which He spoke was not just the effervescence that springs from the buoyancy of youth or from the absence of trouble, for joy and sorrow can, and often do, coexist. Paul speaks of the possibility of being ''sorrowful yet always rejoicing'' (2 Corinthians 6:10). It is striking that James exhorts us to ''count it all joy when ye fall into divers temptations,'' rather than when we fall out of them (James 1:2, KJV).*

This divinely bestowed joy is not just carefree merriment, although it may have that element. It is ''joy in the Holy Spirit,'' and is referred to by Paul as the ''fruit of the Spirit'' (Galatians 5:22), who delights to impart to us the very joy of Christ.

The disciples must have received a severe jolt when Jesus said to them: ''Blessed are you when men hate you, and ostracize you and cast insults at you, and spurn your name as evil, for the sake of the Son of Man. *Be glad in that day, and leap for joy,* for behold, your reward is great in heaven'' (Luke 6:22-23, italics added). That is a rather rugged prescription for joy that will jolt us also, if we think through the implications, and yet it has brought the experience of ''joy inexpressible and full of glory'' (1 Peter 1:8) to countless thousands who have put it to the test.

So even amid the very real limitations, frustrations, and pains of old age, the joy of the Lord can be our experience and our strength (Nehemiah 8:10). ''The cure for age is interest and enthusiasm and work,'' wrote the blind George Matheson in his *Gathered Gems*. ''Life's evening will take its character from the day which has preceded it. Thou shalt always have joy in the evening if thou hast spent the day well.''[3]

The joy of achievement is open to the aging, even though it may be on a more modest scale than of yore. When we cease being self-

*King James Version.

occupied, we will find that new areas of joyous experience will open to us. Making oneself freely available to others, for example, being ingenious in discovering ways of showing kindness and love to others, will prove to be exciting sources of joy.

With less pressure on his time, the older person can discover to a degree never before possible the joy of Bible study and can develop a systematic prayer life that could make the whole world his parish. With more time available, he can find joy in a growing appreciation of music, or art, or literature. There is time now to enjoy in leisurely fashion the wonders of God's creation and induce it to yield some of its fascinating secrets.

Joy can be experienced even in the triumph over pain and physical limitation — or over weakness when our physical powers are on the wane. My father once suffered an accident and was in great pain, but at the same time he was enjoying the presence of the Lord. When I asked him one day how the pain was, he replied, "I can't tell which is the greater, the pain or the glory."

We will get much more positive enjoyment out of the present if we refuse to spoil it by murmuring about the disappointments of the past or harboring unwarranted fears for the future.

A sense of humor and the ability to laugh at oneself can be a valuable asset in coping with the new, and sometimes embarrassing, situations in which we are likely to find ourselves with increasing frequency. Nor should we take it amiss should others sometimes laugh at our quandaries.

CREDITS AND DEBITS

Although there are credits as well as debits in the eventide of life, it is usually the debits that are given prominence, while the credits are largely ignored. Each stage of life has its peculiar testings, but it brings also its own rewards. Old age is no exception to that rule.

The child is relatively carefree and happy; but even childhood knows fear and crushing disappointment. Youth thrills with the excitement of new areas of experience, but young people are often confused, and haunted by fear of the future. Middle age knows the joys of achievement and the sweets of authority; but it knows as well the burden of ever-widening responsibilities.

Old age, with all its acknowledged handicaps and limitations can, however, open up new horizons of joyous possibility to us. The very realization of our own finiteness that comes with the gradual waning of our powers affords us the opportunity of proving in our own experience the validity of Paul's paradoxical claim: "When I am weak, then I am strong" (2 Corinthians 12:10). We, too, can know the thrill of discovering that our inadequacy is complemented by God's sufficiency. Paul's conscious weakness made the opening for God to display the perfection of His power (2 Corinthians 12:9).

J. S. Stewart writes,

> This is the answer — that always it is upon human weakness and humiliation, not human strength and confidence, that God chooses to build His Kingdom; and that He can use us, not merely in spite of our ordinariness and helplessness and disqualifying infirmities, but precisely because of them. . . . Nothing can defeat a Church or soul that takes, not its strength, but its weakness, and offers that to be God's weapon. It was the way of William Carey and Francis Xavier and Paul the apostle. "Lord, here is my human weakness: I dedicate it to Thee for Thy glory!" This is the strategy to which there is no retort. This is the victory which overcomes the world.[4]

Here is an area of life in which the elderly can glorify God uniquely and find deep joy. Has He not caused it to be recorded that "God has chosen the weak things of the world to shame the things which are strong" (1 Corinthians 1:27)? He can still achieve His purpose even in the absence of human strength and resource.

We may feel that we are too weak and insignificant to achieve much for God at our time of life, but Paul assures us that He has chosen nonentities to do battle for Him. Our very weakness and dependence open the way for a greater display of His power and grace. Is it not a revolutionary thought that God is willing to use us, not *in spite of* our weakness, but actually *because* of it? Was it not said of the heroes in God's Hall of Fame that "from weakness [they] were made strong" (Hebrews 11:34)?

In God's economy even the lame can "take the prey" (Isaiah 33:23, KJV). Jacob took the prey only after he was lamed, when the sinew of his self-sufficient scheming withered (Genesis 32:25-32).

Contented, now upon my thigh
    I halt, till life's short journey end;
All helplessness, all weakness, I
    On Thee alone for strength depend;
Nor have I power from Thee to move,
Thy nature and Thy name is love.

Lame as I am I take the prey,
    Hell, earth and sin with ease o'ercome;
I leap for joy, pursue my way,
    And as a bounding hart fly home;
Through all eternity to prove,
Thy nature and Thy name is love.

Charles Wesley

The story of the conflict between Joshua and the Amalekites (Exodus 17:8-16) gives an encouraging parabolic illustration of the joy of intercessory ministry that is open to the weak octogenarians. In the fluctuations of that battle, the key to final victory was not in the hands of Joshua and his army battling in the valley, but in those of Moses and Aaron and Hur—all octogenarians—on the mountaintop. As long as Moses held aloft his rod—symbol of his divinely given authority—the battle swayed in favor of Israel. But when from sheer weariness he allowed it to fall, victory turned to defeat.

As William Cowper put it:

When Moses stood with arms spread wide,
    Success was found on Israel's side,
But when through weariness they failed,
    That moment Amalek prevailed.

It proved to be the *weaponless hands of prayer* on the mountain rather than the clash of arms in the valley that controlled the tides of battle. When Moses could no longer stand, he sat. When he could no longer hold his hands up, Aaron and Hur on either side held them aloft until victory was complete.

Old as they were, those three were young enough to be God's hidden instruments in victory. *Old people can pray,* and prayer is more powerful than arms. Through the ministry of intercession and the exercise of their spiritual authority, those old men strengthened the hands of the younger Joshua and his men who were struggling on the battlefront. Is that not a model for our emulation?

Again, a new and sometimes distressing sense of our need and dependence enables us to prove in experience the reality and validity of faith. Faith grows only as it is tested, and old age is one of the crucibles in which the testing takes place. It is through the dark experiences of life rather than in its lightsome joys that our faith rises to new heights. Such experiences will develop in us a more restful confidence in our heavenly Father's love and providential care.

> When through fiery trials thy pathway shall lie,
> My grace all-sufficient shall be thy supply;
> The flame shall not hurt thee, I only design
> Thy dross to consume and Thy gold to refine.
>
> E'en down to old age all My people shall prove
> My sovereign, eternal, unchangeable love;
> And then, when grey hairs shall their temples adorn,
> Like lambs they shall still in My bosom be borne.
>
> George Keith

With advancing years there comes maturing wisdom, a wisdom that develops only with age. Such wisdom cannot be gleaned from textbooks. No college course can provide it. It must be hammered out, often painfully, on the anvil of real life experience. In our old age we have the privilege of sharing with others our dearly-bought discoveries.

We can with Job, for example, experience the joy of mastering the art of accepting the bitter with the sweet. In the midst of his holocaust of trouble Job's wife urged him to "curse God and die" (Job 2:9) and thus escape further trials. Job's magnificent acceptance of the will of God not only silenced her, but also vindicated God's confidence in him and defeated the devil. It provided succeeding generations with a glowing example of unquestioning confidence in a God whom Job knew to be absolutely trustworthy.

Hear Job's noble reply: "He said to her, 'You speak as one of the foolish women speaks. Shall we indeed accept good from God and not accept adversity?' " (Job 2:10). His faith reached its highest point when Job cried, "Though He slay me, yet I will hope in Him" (Job 13:15).

And the outcome of his trials? "The Lord restored the fortunes of Job . . . And the Lord blessed the latter days of Job more than his beginning" (Job 42:10-12). It is the ending that matters. We are always enriched and never impoverished by an unwavering trust in God.

> As I grow older, Lord, I pray
>   Not for more wisdom, gold or power
>   But that I may know, each passing hour
> A stronger faith as skies grow grey.
>
> Ere ends the pathway, life-long trod —
>   When I can hear the Boatman's oars —
>   I only ask between two shores,
> More faith in God, more faith in God.

L. Mitchell

NOTES

1. Alfons Deeken, *Growing Old* (New York: Paulist, 1972), p. 4.
2. Henry Durbanville, *The Best Is Yet to Be* (Edinburgh: B. McCall Barbour 1950), p. 24.
3. George Matheson, *Gathered Gems* (London: Epworth, 1955), p. 153.
4. J. S. Stewart, *Thine Is the Kingdom* (Edinburgh: St. Andrew, 1956), pp. 23-24.

2

Myths About Old Age

Around the mysterious experience of old age there flutters a flock of predatory myths that need to be frightened away.

A myth is a traditional story evolved or created out of an idea; something fabulous, having no existence in fact. There are many such myths that have become associated with old age which have no factual bases, but that are generally accepted uncritically.

It is a proved fact that if a statement is repeated often enough by a considerable number of people, it comes to be accepted ultimately as truth, whether or not it can be substantiated. Some myths about old age should be exposed and discarded, for they have clouded the closing years of many people who could have been really enjoying growing old with God. Here are some of the myths to which reference will be made in succeeding chapters:

It is a myth that —

- The closing years of life will inevitably be less enjoyable and stimulating than earlier years.
- Memory inexorably declines with age.
- Old people are intrinsically less robust physically and mentally in their later years.
- Old age is a disease and is synonymous with disability and ill health.
- Old age is inevitably a time of decline, and further growth and development are not to be expected.
- The ability to change or to absorb new ideas or learn new skills necessarily diminishes with age.
- Old age is a time of unmitigated misery, and it is normal for old people to be unhappy.
- New relationships are difficult or even impossible to form and maintain in old age.

19

- The passage of time is of itself an accurate index of the changes and capacities of the aging.
- There is an established scientific basis for arbitrarily fixing the compulsory retirement age at sixty-five.
- Old age necessarily results in incontinence.
- The plight of the widower is less poignant than that of the widow.
- Most homes for the elderly are gloomy and prisonlike in atmosphere.
- Uninhibited joy and enjoyment cannot be expected in old age.

Those conclusions may well be challenged, for they do not express the experience of many. In subsequent pages I have endeavored to show that although some of those myths have a real and painful basis for some people, in many cases old age *per se* is not the villain of the piece. The root cause of the unhappy condition is not the outcome of old age, but of other conditions such as disease, which attacks young and old without discrimination.

It is a myth, for example, that all homes and institutions for the elderly are lugubrious and doleful places. One aging missionary friend strenuously resisted any suggestion that he should enter the beautifully appointed and well-staffed home for retired missionaries provided by his mission. His concept of such places was almost, ''All hope abandon, ye who enter here.''

Later, however, physical infirmity left him no option, and reluctantly he became a resident. A year or two afterward, he told me that his experience had been the exact reverse of his expectations. ''How mistaken I was,'' he exclaimed. ''I have never been in a place where we had so much holy fun.''

Some homes and institutions may merit such strictures, but there are very many in which those who are being cared for have every comfort and really enjoy the release from burdens previously carried. They find congenial companionship and rejoice in the freedom from care those sacrificially staffed homes make possible.

3

Senescence Is Not Senility

When is one old? When Bernard Baruch was in his eighties, he was asked when old age takes place. He replied, "Old age is fifteen years older than I am!" His whimsical answer will not satisfy everyone, but it displayed an enviable mind-set toward the aging process.

Is old age a disease such as arthritis, or is it, like infancy, a normal stage in human life? Is it a state of body or of mind?

Aging is a slow biological change that inexorably overtakes us all. *Senescence* is the term used to describe the state of growing old. It should, however, be distinguished from *senility,* which is the weakness or debility that stems from old age. The two are by no means synonymous. Many who are experiencing senescence are very far from being senile. Aging is not the same as being old; aging is a process, and being old is a state of mind.

Senescence may be defined as the process in which the self-regulating mechanisms of the body begin to fail.[1] It affects people in different ways. It is in part a state of mind, for there are many elderly people who are very youthful in spirit, and there are some young people who are old at twenty-five. As with other stages of life, senescence has its own peculiar needs and recognizable characteristics.

Old age does not begin at any particular chronological age. So gradual is its onset that often it is hardly noticed. The first gray hairs are always something of a surprise. As has been said, we age minute by minute, not year by year.

One elderly lady of one hundred years, when asked about the made of her life in general, replied, "Can't tell yet, I'm still making my life."

The Jews had their own standard of measurement for the aging

21

process. They viewed it as coming in three stages. From sixty to seventy they regarded as the commencement of old age; from seventy to eighty as hoary-headed old age; and from eighty on as advanced old age, or in biblical language, "well stricken in years." That arbitrary division may be convenient, but it cannot be said to be scientifically accurate.

> It is not the years that make men old,
>   The spirit may be young
> Though three-score years and ten
>   The wheels of life have run —
> God has Himself recorded
>   In His blessed Word of truth,
> That they who wait upon the Lord,
>   These shall renew their youth.[2]
>
> Anonymous

In Oriental culture, age is equated with wisdom. In countries like Japan, the elderly have a respected status and enjoy high prestige. A person is valued for his intrinsic character more than for what he achieves. Our culture adopts a more utilitarian stance. Achievement and productivity tend to be given first place, and in practice, quality of life is regarded as of secondary importance. There is little doubt on which side the Bible stands on the issue.

There is a great degree of truth in the old adage that one is just as old as he feels. Morton Puner maintains that "Most people over seventy are secretly young, disguised in an old skin. The aging and old do not think of themselves as old . . . Underneath that aging skin and body, they feel as young as ever."[3] Old age is a relative term, and most feel younger than their official age.

While the aging process is largely beyond their control, it must be admitted that many of the problems of the elderly are self-inflicted and could be solved, in measure at least, if they were resolutely attacked.

There are some, for example, who feel they are of little social significance — no one needs or wants them. But often it is their own negative attitude toward themselves that prevents their being needed and wanted. To correct that, a new mind-set is demanded. In the biblical view, no one is insignificant and valueless. Did not our Lord say that to gain the whole world at the cost of one's soul would be a bad bargain (Mark 8:36)? We should learn to view the potential of our lives as God views it.

> If you no longer look ahead,
> If your ambition's fires are dead,
> Then you're an old man.

Dr. F.B. Meyer, himself an octogenarian, had this to say to a group of people who were entering their eightieth year:

> Don't allow yourself to feel old; don't give up your interest in life; cultivate a hobby; have a game now and then with your grandchildren, or someone else's; don't think about the end — God has lovingly planned that, and you will be as unaware of your passing out as you were of your coming in. I take it for granted, of course, that you have entrusted yourself to Christ for eternity. . . .
>
> I am very conscious of my unworthiness and failure. I know not where I should stand, if it were not for the Blood of the Cross, and the Mediatorship of the throne.
>
> My outlook for the next world is summed up in the words, "His servants shall serve Him." If I had a hundred lives, they should be at Christ's disposal. In His service is perfect freedom.

Technically, old age is not something of which one dies. The cause of death is disease, or organic deterioration as a result of the body's failing to replace vital cells. This inevitable process is no surprise to God. His cosmic plan makes adequate provision for the needs of people at every stage of life.

> They call it going down the hill
> When we are growing old;
> And speak with mournful accents
> When our years are nearly told.
> They sigh when talking of the past,
> The days that used to be —
> As if the future were not bright
> With immortality.[4]

Anonymous

SEVEN AGES OF MAN?

In his play *As You Like It* [act 2, sc. 7], Shakespeare defined in cryptic and caustic language what he conceived to be the Seven Ages of Man:

> . . . At first the infant,
> Mewling and puking in the nurse's arms:
> Then the whining schoolboy, with his satchel,
> And shining morning face, creeping like snail
> Unwillingly to school: and then the lover,
> Sighing like furnace, with a woeful ballad
> Made to his mistress' eyebrow: Then a soldier;
> Full of strange oaths, and bearded like the pard,
> Jealous in honour, sudden and quick in quarrel,
> Seeking the bubble reputation
> Even in the cannon's mouth. And then the justice,
> In fair round belly with good capon lin'd,
> With eyes severe and beard of formal cut,
> Full of wise saws and modern instances,
> And so he plays his part: The sixth age shifts
> Into the lean and slippered pantaloon,
> With spectacles on nose, and pouch on side;
> His youthful hose well sav'd, a world too wide
> For his shrunk shank, and his big manly voice,
> Turning again towards childish treble, pipes
> And whistles in his sound. Last scene of all,
> That ends this strange eventful history,
> Is second childishness, and mere oblivion,
> Sans teeth, sans eyes, sans taste, sans everything.

Whether or not Shakespeare's analysis is valid, there are three easily differentiated kinds of ages of man, although they may be widely disparate. Varying terminology is adopted by different sociologists, but the simplest classification would be *chronological age* — the measurement of age by our time standards; *physiological age* — reflected in one's vital functions and physical condition; and *psychological age* — gauged by the way one feels and acts or reacts to people and circumstances.

Between those three there may be considerable disparity, and the same person can have three different ages, according to the criteria adopted. People of the same chronological age may act quite differently.

It is unwise to think of age merely in terms of clock and calendar, for many who are chronologically old are psychologically young, and vice versa. When we reach the magical age of sixty-five, there is no sharp and visible decline in our ability to function mentally or physically simply because we have reached the compulsory retiring age. And yet some act as if that were the case. Indeed, there are specialists in the field of gerontology who maintain that most old people are intrinsically far more capable and robust physically and mentally than we have tended to believe.

Our powers and capacities do not deteriorate overnight simply because we reach a certain age, for chronological age is not necessarily the root cause of a decline in efficiency; nor should it be used as a yardstick to determine what or how much we should do. Other factors must be taken into account. Although we grow slower in some ways with age, in other ways we may grow quicker. To be ten years older is not synonymous with being ten years less active or useful to society.

It is true that the elderly can grow mentally arthritic and become rigid and inflexible in their ways; but the causes of that condition may be quite different from the number of years lived. Often it is the result of a voluntary opting out of activity and involvement, relinquishing the struggle for further growth and development. Of itself, old age is not a reason for doing less, but it does provide a convenient excuse if one is desired.

One of the very popular biographies of a generation ago was *Lax of Poplar,* the story of a Methodist minister who achieved fantastic success in ministering to the socially underprivileged in the slum area of Poplar in London.

When he was himself growing old, he maintained that there were two kinds of age — age of body and age of mind — and that the latter largely governed the former. He wrote,

> The age of the body depends on the vital organs, the heart, the lungs and the like. These are "set" for a certain period. They may get worn out, either by fair wear and tear, or much sooner by unfair wear and tear. You cannot help that.
>
> But you can control the age of your mind. You can, if you face life in the right spirit, keep the mind young almost indefinitely. And

remember that the mind controls the activities and energies of all the rest of the body. It is the supreme organ. If you let the mind grow old, the body will grow old also. How are you to keep the mind young? The most important thing is to cultivate a cheerful spirit. . . .

And keep an open active mind . . . The moment a man loses his sense of wonder . . . he becomes old.[5]

NOTES

1. Morton Puner, *To the Good, Long Life* (London: Macmillan, 1974), p. 99.
2. From George Henderson, *Heaven's Cure for Earth's Care* (London: G. F. Vallance, n.d.), p. 37.
3. Puner, p. 7.
4. Henderson, p. 37.
5. William Henry Lax, *Lax of Poplar* (London: Epworth, 1927).

4

An Aging Community

When he was Secretary to the United Nations Organization, U Thant referred to Asia as "a continent that has grown phenomenally young." In most Asian churches the young predominate. The same cannot be said of the Western nations. While Asia faces the acute problem posed by the preponderance of the young, the West has to solve the equally serious problem of a rapidly growing proportion of aging people.

In 1850, only 2.5 percent of American citizens were over sixty-five. Today the proportion is 10 percent. Ten years ago, 4.4 percent were seventy-five years old or over. By the year 2000 the number could reach 6.9 percent.[1] The United States today has 25 million people of sixty-five and over. If the present tendency toward a decreasing death rate continues, the number could increase to 38 million by the year 2000. The United States is not alone in this dilemma, as similar conditions exist in Europe.

Among the problems arising out of this significant social shift and growing imbalance is that of providing nursing homes and institutions for the care of the elderly. The position of the United States gives an indication of the growing concern of those responsible.

There are now 1.3 million elderly American citizens who are living in such homes. At the current rate of increase, the number will exceed 2 million by 2000. The provision of accommodation for the additional number will add considerably to the financial burdens of the younger income earners.

A Gallup Poll reported in *Christianity Today* (21 May 1980) revealed that not all persons of fifty and over are worried about the future. Fifty-nine percent described their outlook over the next twenty years as either "optimistic," or "very optimistic," while only 30 percent said "pessimistic," or "very pessimistic."

27

In many other cultures, particularly Asian, grandparents were cared for by their families until death. Today, even in eastern lands, that is growing more difficult. With a much longer life-expectancy — up to fifteen years longer for a woman — the magnitude of the problems to be faced in the next decade is mind-boggling. Longevity combines with inflation to make serious inroads into the real income of people.

It is interesting to note, however, that even in the current attitude to the aged and aging, the winds of change are blowing strongly. In an article entitled "Grey Power Flexes its Muscles," Kerry Wakefield makes some astute observations concerning developments on the Australian scene.

Concerning a protest alleging that Mr. Justice Norris was too old to conduct an inquiry into the operation of the media in Australia, Wakefield wrote:

> Never fear, Mr. Justice Norris. The whippersnapper who said that at 77 you are too old to run the media inquiry, is out of touch. The future lies in wrinkly hands. Old age is on the way in.
>
> Some people predict that the greying Australian society will lead to a new respect for the aged, and a swing from hedonism and individualism, towards family values and responsibility.
>
> The managing director of the *Ibis Research Services Ltd,* Mr. Phil Ruthven says: "In less than five years you will see a new-found respect for experience, firmness, discipline, and age. The social lop-sidedness that the youth cult produced is vanishing . . . the 'me' syndrome will be replaced by the 'we' syndrome.
>
> The reasons for these forecast social changes lie in the growing numbers of middle-aged or old people in Australia. By 1986, for the first time, more Australians will be over the age of 30 than under the age of 30. And while one person in eleven is now over 65, by the year 2000, it will be one in eight. . . . [2]

In view of those rather alarming facts, the church and its leaders are under obligation to review their past performance and to prepare for future reality. Generally speaking, the aged form the group least imaginatively catered for in the church's program. It should not be left to the sociologists and government to take the initiative. The church can play an invaluable part in restoring biblical standards of family life and encouraging the solidarity of the family.

Generation Gap

There has always been a generation gap between the old and the young. It is not something that has suddenly developed, although the present generation has seen it widen perceptibly. The plain fact is that, whether they recognize it or not, both youth and age need each other. Mutual cross-fertilization — both intellectual and spiritual — can result in great mutual enrichment.

One of the oldest pieces of writing extant is in a museum in Istanbul. It reads, "Alas, times are not what they used to be. Children no longer obey their parents."[3] How strangely contemporary! History does indeed repeat itself. It seems that neither youth nor age is essentially different in its outlook and relationships from the way it was thousands of years ago. Radical youth has always challenged and clashed with conservative age. Youth demands change; age clings to the *status quo,* and each tends to be intolerant of the other. Genuine tolerance and Christian love and patience are needed. Lack of those virtues is at the root of a great deal of juvenile delinquency.

Youth is impatient; sometimes the old are intransigent. Youth is radical; age veers toward conservatism. But each would be much poorer without the other. Each has its own distinctive and necessary contribution to make to home, church, and society.

This anonymous prayer could well be offered regularly by both old and young:

> Lord, make old people tolerant,
> Young folk sympathetic,
> Great folk humble,
> Busy folk patient,
> Bad folk good,
> And make me what I ought to be.

There are, unfortunately, too many situations in the contemporary world in which young people behave very cruelly toward the aged. For such behavior there is no excuse. Sadistic violence against the old and infirm has become too common a feature of city life to be ignored. On the other hand, there are a great number of young people — probably the majority — who are kind and considerate, and who get along very well with those older than themselves.

Sometimes an even closer bond exists between children and grandparents than between children and parents. One reason may be that the former, because they have no responsibility for exercising discipline, are more indulgent toward their grandchildren than they were to their own children. That makes the kind and indulgent grandparent very popular, but if care is not exercised, it could cause tension with the parents.

In speaking of the kingdom of heaven, Jesus used the illustration of "the head of a household, who brings forth out of his treasure things new and old" (Matthew 13:52). Both old and young can have something of value from their own experience to contribute to the common good.

Youth and age are not necessarily antithetical; each can complement the other. Often a very young spirit inhabits a very old body. And some young people have very wise heads on young shoulders.

Dr. Thomas Guthrie of Scotland once said, "They say I am growing old because my hair is silvered, and there are crowsfeet on my forehead, and my step is not as firm and elastic as before. But they are mistaken; that is not me. The knees are weak, but they are not me. The brow is wrinkled, but the brow is not me. This is the house I live in, but I am young, younger than I ever was before."

Do what we like, we cannot escape growing old. But we can keep young in spirit and outlook if we steadfastly set out to do so. Dickens's Sam Weller said of Mr. Pickwick, "Blest if I don't think his heart was born twenty-five years after his body!" Most of us have known some choice souls who had that quality in common with Mr. Pickwick. "Within every old person is a young one, or at least a middle-aged one, trying to escape the idea of old age."

In a fifteenth-century religious lyric, this transition from youth to age is treated.

> From the time we are born
> Our youth passeth from day to day,
> And age increaseth more and more;
> And so it now, the sooth to say,
> At every hour a point is less,
> So fast goeth our youth away,
> And youth will come again no more.
> But age will make us both pale and grey,

Therefore take heed, both night and day,
How fast our youth doth pass away.
And both young and old, let us pray
That God send patience in our old age.

NOTES

1. Editorial, *Christianity Today,* 2 May 1980, p. 12.
2. Kerry Wakefield, "Grey Power Flexes its Muscles," *Melbourne Age,* 28 October 1980.
3. E. Stanley Jones, *Mastery* (London: Hodder & Stoughton, 1950), p. 60.

5

Be Prepared!

When should preparation for the joys and exigencies of old age commence? Each stage of life, in a sense, is a preparation for the next. What we are and do now will have a formative effect on our future.

An enjoyable and fruitful old age is not automatic. It must be prepared for and worked at. Yet many of us in earlier life — myself among the number — have given little serious thought to this important aspect of our lives. The days were full, the present was pressing and fascinating, and we left the future to take care of itself.

Now the years have caught up on us, and some have discovered that they have begun their retirement years unprepared. Now they wish they had taken time to prepare for the changes that inevitably come. Not all have mastered the art of using leisure in an enjoyable, yet rewarding, manner. We should, therefore, encourage younger people not to repeat our mistake.

Those who in earlier years have maintained mental interests such as reading will be less at a disadvantage when bodily functions become impaired, than those who have not cultivated this aspect of their lives. But it is never too late to begin anew, provided there is a positive attitude and a firm purpose.

The adage "an old dog cannot be taught new tricks" is one of the myths associated with old age that should be exposed and discarded. It will take longer to acquire new skills — but that will be more through fear of failure than lack of ability. Research at the Duke University Center for the Study of the Aging found "the slowing down" proved to be caused by unconscious anxiety. When drugs that counteracted anxiety were taken improved performance resulted.

The elderly can do many things. New learning skills can be acquired quite late in life. Fear that one is too old, not lack of brain power, prevents people from making the attempt. "New tricks" take

33

longer to learn because the brain and nervous system tend to slow down.

Toward the end of her life my wife was suffering from multiple sclerosis. The trouble first appeared in her hands, and gradually she lost the use of thumb and first finger. Before this time she had never attempted painting, but with encouragement, she took it up and found she had quite an unusual gift. When she lost the use of her thumb and finger, she used the remaining ones. Her work was of such quality that she was admitted as a member of the Fellowship of Artists. When she became so limited that she could do little else, she was still able to paint. During the two years of her illness, she completed forty or fifty paintings that are treasured by relatives and friends. How many other old people may have similar hidden talents that could be uncovered if only there was the encouragement to discover it, and "give it a go."

As Karl Menninger put it, feeling that it is too late for improving our old age, or that we can't do things any more, can become an alibi for not doing the things we can do. To say "What's the good, it's too late" is a counsel of despair. Furthermore, the Christian has supernatural aid available to enable him to do all God's will. "I can do all things through Him who strengthens me" (Philippians 4:13).

A MAN CAN GROW

Specialists in this field are unified in holding that apart from serious illness or other adverse physical conditions, *the normal human being can learn to grow at any age.* Basically intelligent people will normally remain so, even though the mental processes may slow down.

An Army intelligence test that had been given to a group of men in their youth was given to the same group forty-two years later. The result? They returned an increased score. So even when bodily functions are growing more feeble, growth is still possible.

> Thank God! A man can grow!
> He is not bound
> With earthward gaze to creep along the ground:
> Though his beginning be but poor and low
> Thank God! A man can grow!
>
> Author Unknown

Well-recognized laws of mental and spiritual growth — if we are sufficiently interested to comply with them — will be operative right to the end of life, albeit at a slower pace. Ambition need not be the prerogative of only the young or middle-aged. In point of fact, we do not grow old with age, we age because we are not growing.

After a prolonged illness, my first wife was dying of cancer. About ten days before the end, I was attending her, trying to make things as easy and comfortable for her as possible. She was well aware that the end was near.

Turning to me she said, "Don't make things too easy for me, dear. I must keep on growing." She might well have been preoccupied with her own sufferings. Instead, the consistent pattern of a lifetime of walking with God asserted itself — to continue growing in likeness to Christ. That ambition persisted and blossomed right to the end.

Despite our age, we can — and must — keep growing spiritually. Inward growth is still possible after the physical falls into decay, for true growth is mental and spiritual. It is possible for us to be intellectually and spiritually voracious and ambitious right to the end.

I recently attended the diamond wedding of a very dear friend who is blind. Through more than fifty years we have enjoyed a close friendship. One of his most notable characteristics is that he has an insatiable appetite for the truth of God. For new material he is largely dependent on what is read to him, but at eighty-five he is as mentally avid and alert as when I first met him. He is a glowing example of the claim that the best indication of growth is an expanding mind, and an eagerness for truth.

Dr. E. Stanley Jones, as an old man, was a fine illustration of his own teaching. He suggested the following steps for continuing growth in old age:

1. Don't retire. Change your occupation . . . to something you have always wanted to do.
2. Learn something new every day.
3. Set yourself to be gracious to someone every day.
4. Don't let yourself grow negative; be positive.
5. Look around you for something for which to be grateful every day. Gratitude will become a settled habit.
6. Now that your bodily activities are slowing down, let your spiritual

activities increase. Old age provides increased opportunity for prayer.

7. Keep laying up as the years come and go "the good store" of which Jesus spoke. This "good store" is the depository of every thought, motive, action, attitude which we drop into the subconscious mind. It can be the deep subsoil into which we can strike our roots in old age and blossom at the end like a night-blooming cereus.[1]

Our basic intelligence becomes no greater after early teen age, but neither does it necessarily diminish significantly until late in life. We do, however, discover how to make better use of our mental powers through learning and experience. This can continue to the end, and our knowledge can develop and mature into wisdom.

THE OLDER THE BETTER

It has been claimed, and with good reason, that the older one is — provided faculties have not become seriously impaired — the better one is intellectually. Vision becomes wider, opinions more mature, and outlook wiser and more realistic.

Indeed, there are figures to show that the most productive period of life lies nearer its end than its beginning, especially between the ages of sixty and seventy.

The results of a study made of four hundred noted men of all times and in differing spheres of activity were reported in *Sunshine Magazine*. It revealed some striking results. It was found that 35 percent of the world's greatest achievements were by people in the sixty-seventy age bracket. A further 23 percent were by those between seventy and eighty. The octogenarian group accounted for a further 6 percent. No less than 64 percent of the world's greatest achievements were accomplished by people over sixty years of age.

Gilles Lambert maintained that "the over 60's are the best reservoir of talent and energy in the nation." Ramsey Clark, one-time US Attorney-General, remarked that he would not trade "fifteen Alexanders at 21, or William Pitts at 23, for one Oliver Wendell Holmes at 80, in terms of human value."[2]

These findings are solid comfort and encouragement to us as we face the future.

Because our bodily functions and capacities do suffer wear and tear, Shakespeare's uncharitable caricature in his Seven Ages of Man previously quoted may be true of some, but it need by no means be true of all.

There are no rigid, clear-cut, inexorable seven ages of man. No two people age at exactly the same rate, nor does the process follow the same pattern. For some it takes much longer than for others who were originally endowed with greater vigor and drive, qualities that help to retard the ravages of age.

No matter where the reader may be in the chronological age scale, much can still be done to prepare for a more enjoyable and satisfying life in the years that remain. One can be creative right until the end of life as has been abundantly demonstrated, even though the canvas may grow smaller. Grandma Moses attained worldwide fame when she took up her career as an artist after the age of seventy-five.

In order to make a success of old age, one must begin it earlier rather than postponing it! But even if we have neglected to do so, we can still make it better than if we did nothing about it. Let us accept the stirring challenge of William Carey's motto: "Attempt great things for God; expect great things from God" (Isaiah 54:2).

In concluding his book, *Growing Old,* Robert Kastenbaum, professor of Psychology at the University of Massachusetts, had this to say concerning his own outlook on approaching old age.

> There was a time in my own life when I wondered about the value of growing and being old. No more. I do not want to miss my old age any more than I would choose to have skipped childhood or adolescence. But I do feel an increased sense of responsibility to this future self, and to all those whose lives may cross my path. What kind of old man will I be, given the chance? The answer to that question depends largely on the kind of person I am right now. For growing old is an ongoing project of self-actualisation through the lifespan.[3]

LIFE BEGINS AT EIGHTY

A Canadian member of the China Inland Mission, Benjamin Ririe by name, retired from missionary work when he reached seventy years of age, and settled in Toronto. When he was eighty, he decided to learn New Testament Greek, as he had not had the opportunity when he was younger. He became proficient in reading the Greek New Testament.

At the age of ninety, he undertook a refresher course in Greek at a Baptist seminary in Toronto. When he had reached the age of one hundred, he was at a meeting at which I was speaking. In his pocket was a small, well-worn Greek lexicon, which he used to brush up his Greek while traveling on the subway! He was still effervescent with a desire to be his mental best for God, even though he was a centenarian.

Canon C. H. Nash, who founded the Melbourne Bible Institute and trained a thousand young men and women for Christian service, retired from his principalship at the age of seventy.

When he was eighty he told me that he had received assurance from the Lord that a further ten years of fruitful ministry lay ahead of him. That assurance was abundantly fulfilled. Until he was ninety-one, Canon Nash was uniquely blessed in a ministry of Bible teaching to key groups of clergy and laymen — undoubtedly the most fruitful years of his very fruitful life. When he was ninety, I found him completing — with much enjoyment — the reading of volume 6 of Toynbee's monumental history for mental exercise! Like Caleb, he defied the natural order, and continued to increase in stature to the end.

E. Stanley Jones at seventy tells of receiving the assurance from God: " 'I am going to give you the best ten years of your life.' One of those years is gone, and it has literally been the very best. So I expect the next nine years to be the same — or better." His expectation was fully realized.

THE GIFT OF FRIENDSHIP

The ability to make and maintain enduring friendships is one of the best ways of preparing for the inevitable tests of old age. To have the love and support of tried friends and their prayer fellowship in times of trial is something that cannot be bought with money.

There is more than a grain of truth in the saying that you can tell a man by his friends. And friends are never so precious and appreciated as when we grow older. As the circle narrows, the close friends of earlier years who shared much of our own background and experience are especially valued. The best friends in old age are usually those whose friendship has been cultivated in earlier years.

Some, like Paul the apostle, have a genius for friendship, whereas others find it exceedingly difficult to establish and maintain a close and intimate relationship. But that need not always be so. Prayer, and a willingness to take the first step in making an approach, will often be richly rewarded. Of course this is a problem that should have been faced and dealt with in earlier years, but better late than never.

As our older friends pass on before us, we should not rule out the possibility of forging new bonds of friendship and fellowship with younger people who will help to keep our viewpoint youthful. The lovely friendship of Paul the aged with young Timothy is a classic example of a satisfying friendship between old and young. How enriching it was for Timothy, and what a comfort he was to Paul the aged!

Friendliness begets friendship. It is a two-way relationship, and must be worked at. The shy person finds it difficult to make the first approach to someone else — but should one always expect the other person to take the initiative? Friendships are forged on the anvil of shared confidences; we must be willing to open ourselves up to others if we expect them to reciprocate. We all have something to share that could enrich the lives of others.

It was sound advice that Polonius gave to his son: "Those friends thou hast, and their adoption tried, grapple them to thy soul with hooks of steel" (*Hamlet,* act 1, sc. 3). Solomon said that "a friend loves at all times," but he later added, "There is a friend who sticks closer than a brother" (Proverbs 17:17; 18:24).

The true quality of friendship shines through as we approach old age. The superficial fall away, but the true friend sticks. But even when earthly friends fail us, we have the assured presence of our Heavenly Friend right to the end of the age.

NOTES

1. E. Stanley Jones, *Growing Spiritually* (Nashville: Abingdon, 1953), p. 313.
2. Morton Puner, *To the Good, Long Life* (London: Macmillan, 1974), p. 26.
3. Robert Kastenbaum, *Growing Old* (Melbourne: Nelson, 1979), p. 121.

6

Attitudes, Not Arteries

Attitudes toward old age vary greatly because people are so diverse in temperament and outlook. Some face the prospect of growing old in a negative manner, and their reactions are consequently set in a minor key. Others, however, have a positive outlook, and they strike more major chords.

The former group are preoccupied with the undeniably real disabilities and disadvantages that often cloud old age, whereas the latter, without ignoring those difficulties, see beyond them to the opportunities, possibilities, and compensations that senior status can bring.

An interesting fact emerges from a study of such cases — those in the latter category include many who are most seriously disabled, or suffer the greatest pain. They have somehow learned to tap sources of strength that enable them to rise above their handicaps and live lives of great usefulness.

Those cheerful souls with a positive outlook have embraced the strengthening truth that "the will of God" — which includes the aging process — "is good and acceptable and perfect" (Romans 12:2). They take those words in their fullest and most literal sense as being true *in their case*. And that makes all the difference.

It is one thing to accept some alleged fact as being *theoretically* true. It is quite another, in practical terms, to accept it as true *in one's own case* and to act upon it. It is only logical that if God's will is good and acceptable and perfect, then complaining about it or rebelling against it is out. If God's will is acceptable, it must be accepted. If it is perfect, it cannot be improved upon. When it is accepted from the heart, serenity ensues. This is not mere theory, but solid fact that has been proved in innumerable cases.

This wholesome attitude has been reflected in many well-known lives, among them John Quincy Adams, one of the early Presidents of the United States.

41

When he was very old, someone asked him how he was. He returned this quizzical answer: "Thank you, John Quincy Adams is very well himself, sir, but the house in which he lives is falling to pieces. Time and seasons have nearly destroyed it. The roof is well-worn, the walls shattered. It trembles with every gale. I think John Quincy Adams will soon have to move out. But he himself is very well."[1]

We all know that old age is as inevitable as the succession of summer and winter, so it is wisdom for us to face the prospect with realism, and yet with optimism. It is in our own interests to have a mind-set that will help get the best out of aging. That attitude will save us from falling into the bleak and gray pessimism that is so common.

As each season has its own peculiar beauty and purpose, so each age has its own attractiveness. "We all do fade as a leaf" (Isaiah 64:6, KJV) says the prophet. But is there anything more beautiful than a scarlet maple leaf in the fall? There can be a rare beauty manifested in the life of an aging Christian who has walked for a lifetime in the light of God's countenance.

Old age is just as important and meaningful a part of God's perfect will as is youth. God is every bit as interested in the old as in the young.

UNDEVELOPED POTENTIAL

There is great potential locked up in the lives of our fine young people; they are one of the most precious assets of the church and should be nurtured and developed. But there is also a great potential, largely untapped, in the accumulated knowledge, experience, and faith of older Christians. The whole work of God will be greatly enriched when more attention is given to releasing and utilizing that hidden resource. Today older people are making a much more valuable contribution on the mission fields of the world than at any time hitherto.

The Bible is essentially a realistic document. It tells things as they really are. Failures are as faithfully reported as are successes. The Master never pictured the road to heaven as primrose-strewn. Browning captured the realism of His Lord when he wrote:

How very hard it is to be a Christian!
Hard for you and me;
Not the mere task of making real
That duty up to its ideal,
Effecting thus complete and whole
A purpose of the human soul
For that is always hard to do.

The Bible is equally realistic in its approach to old age. The writers do not attempt to gloss over its less desirable aspects and accompaniments, but consistently portray the vast contrast between an old age lived in fellowship with God, and one lived without Him.

For some, old age is pleasant and enjoyable; for others, it is painful and depressing. Some anticipate it with eagerness, others with fear and foreboding. Some accept it, others rebel against it. It is among the latter that most unhappiness is found. Some find it exhilarating, others are bored. "I am not as old as my arteries," said one old man, "I am only as old as my attitudes."

That there will be progressive changes in both mind and body is a simple physiological and psychological fact, and we must accept it as such. If we can accept that inevitable change without exaggerating it on the one hand or foolishly trying to ignore it on the other, we will be saving ourselves from many sorrows. To accept old age and what it brings with philosophical realism is the healthiest and most helpful stance.

"The trick in aging," said one, "is to be both realistic and optimistic." It is not a bland, blind optimism that is being advocated in this book. It would be totally untrue to the realities of life to minimize the fact that old age does bring increasing problems and often pain and suffering in its wake. Denying the reality of those problems, as Christian Science advocates, in no way lessens their impact.

The Christian faith, however, brings onto the field a whole battery of spiritual resources that are equally available to all believers. When appropriated, they can enable us to rise above the adverse factors, though the road is, at times, through failure to victory.

LEARNING CONTENTMENT

It is not without significance that Paul said, "*I have learned* to be content in whatever circumstance I am," (Philippians 4:11, italics added). He did not say "I have always been content with any circumstances." For him, as it will be for us, it had been a painful learning process in the school of suffering. The point is that he graduated! It was in the same school that the Son of God learned obedience (Hebrews 5:8).

> Let no one think that sudden in a minute
> All is accomplished, and the work is done,
> Though with thy earliest dawn thou shouldst begin it,
> Scarce were it ended in thy setting sun
>
> F. W. H. Meyers

Our Lord likened the Christian life to a river that broadened, deepened, and gathered volume as it flowed down to the sea — an encouraging picture for the aging Christian. There is no reason why our closing years should not be as enjoyable, stimulating, and fruitful as in earlier life. A life of increasing instead of diminishing, a life of continual outflow, can be ours. Read again Christ's alluring picture:

> Jesus stood and cried out, saying, "If any man is thirsty, let him come to Me and drink. He who believes in Me, as the Scripture said, 'From his innermost being shall flow rivers of living water.' " But this He spoke of the Spirit, whom those who believed in Him were to receive (John 7:37-39).

Such people refuse to concede defeat to Father Time. They resolve to master old age, not to be defeated by it. They accept help from others, but only when it is absolutely necessary. They are grateful, thoughtful, and cheerful in adversity. Their very resilience is a great encouragement to their contemporaries who are incited to discover their secret.

On one occasion, Sylvester Horne, a brilliant preacher of the last generation, preached a sermon to a congregation of elderly people. He was himself in that category. When someone inquired what his text had been, he invited them to make a guess.

"At eventide it shall be light," suggested one.

"No, try again."

"Come unto me, all ye weary, and I will give you rest."

"No" was again the answer.

What was his text? "And about *the eleventh hour* He went

out, . . . [and] He said to them, 'You too go into the vineyard' "
(Matthew 20:6-7, italics added).[2]

Even though many of us have reached our eleventh hour, here is the
Master's challenge and encouragement to us to keep at work for Him
right to the very end. It is not too late to begin even now! Remember
that those who began work at the eleventh hour received exactly the
same remuneration as those who began at dawn. What marvelous
grace!

There are elderly people, however, whose outlook is determinedly
negative and pessimistic. They resent the graying hair and wrinkles,
and in an endeavor to hide their aging from themselves and others,
dress and act as though they were young. But to refuse to grow old is
just as foolish as to refuse to abandon childhood.

A thankful and cheerful outlook on life can make all the difference between enjoyment and misery. We have no choice about
growing old, but the choice of how we spend the aging years is
entirely our own.

How we begin the day can subtly color the succeeding hours. My
father lived with us for some time after we were married. One day my
wife said to me, "You can always tell when grandpa gets up, because
the moment his feet hit the floor he starts to sing." There are worse
ways of beginning the day!

Mr. Harold St. John was a man of singular sweetness of character. I
was much impressed when on one gray morning he concluded his
prayer at family worship on this cheerful note, "And so, Lord, we
step out blithely into the new day." The day itself was gloomy, but
there was no gloom in his outlook.

Most people do not feel at their best first thing in the morning, but
to give room to gloom and misery achieves little. On the other hand,
to deliberately adopt a positive attitude of rejoicing in God goes a long
way toward dispelling the gloom.

The Master set a glowing example of that attitude of mind when He
was on the way to the cross. Having observed the Last Supper with
His disciples, Mark tells us that "after singing a hymn they went out
to the Mount of Olives" (Mark 14:26).

Can we know the hymn that Jesus sang with His disciples? Indeed
we can. It was the Jewish custom to sing Psalm 118 after the Passover
feast, and that was without doubt the hymn they sang. A thoughtful

and reverent reading of the psalm in the light of that will give fresh insights into the glories of the Savior.

When we realize that as Jesus sang the psalm He was actually on the way to the cross, it invests the familiar chorus that we often sing so glibly with new and poignant meaning. "This is the day which the Lord has made; let us rejoice and be glad in it" (Psalm 118:24).

If ever there was an occasion when Jesus would have had reason to be dismayed and self-occupied, that was the time. But instead, He went to the cross with a song of acceptance of God's will on His lips. He has left us an example that we should follow His steps.

IN ACCEPTANCE LIES PEACE

"In acceptance lies peace" is an adage that has gained considerable currency, and not without good reason. It is an entirely biblical concept, and nowhere has it more relevance than in reference to old age.

In a letter I received while writing this chapter, one who was tragically bereaved wrote: "When we want to tear our hearts out with why's, I've been able to come back to those words 'In acceptance lies peace.' It's strange how they've been with me through the years, because they do apply in other situations too."

It is easy to say the words, but not so easy to adopt the attitude. For someone else to say to us, "Old age is something that must just be accepted," is trite and simplistic, for aging is a problem that tends to grow more complex with the years. To accept old age in reality has far-reaching implications. Acceptance is not passively suffering the unavoidable with due resignation. It is saying yes to life in all its areas and with all its problems.

Amy Wilson Carmichael of Dohnavur, India, who achieved great things for God and the Indian people in spite of serious and chronic physical disability, suggests that acceptance always means the happy choice of mind and heart of that which God appoints, because it is His good and acceptable and perfect will.

That is quite different from the attitude of the stoic or the fatalist. Rather that kind of acceptance was reflected in the attitude of Emma Piechynska, wife of a sadistic Polish count. It was written of her, "There was no mournful resignation or melancholy submission about her — Every fresh experience of suffering was a challenge to her will.

Suffering must not be accepted with mere submission. It must be borne deliberately. Every experience is worth what it costs."[3]

Joyful acceptance of the will of God was expressed in these optimistic words by Madame Jeanne de la Mothe Guyon, a French noble-woman who was incarcerated for ten years in the Bastille for her faith.

> A little bird am I,
> Shut out from fields of air,
> Yet in my cage I sit and sing
> To Him who placed me there;
> Well-pleased a prisoner to be,
> Because, O God, it pleaseth Thee.
>
> Naught else have I to do,
> I sing the whole day long,
> And He whom most I love to please
> Doth listen to my song.
> He caught and bound my wandering wing,
> And still He bends to hear me sing.
>
> O, it is good to soar
> These bolts and bars above,
> To Him whose purpose I adore,
> Whose providence I love;
> And in Thy perfect will to find
> The joy, the freedom of the mind.

With an outlook like that, it is not surprising that the authorities were unable to break the spirit of such an indomitable woman.

"I have no desire that my imprisonment should end before the right time," she wrote. "I love my chains. My senses indeed have not any relish for such things, but my heart is separated from them and borne over them."

If we are to know serenity and joy in our closing years, we must gladly accept our age, and lay ourselves out to maintain a positive and cheerful outlook. It should be our fixed ambition to make our last years the best. And why should they not be? Did God not say, "I will do better unto you than at your beginnings" to failing Israel (Ezekiel 36:11, KJV)?

In his book, *Living to Old Age,* Dr. Paul Tournier has a fine chapter on acceptance that would abundantly repay careful study and consideration.[4] The kind of acceptance advocated is not that of apathy and passivity. Mere capitulation to necessity will bring neither serenity nor joy, but realistic acceptance of our age will kindle the purpose to achieve the very best for God and man in the months or years that remain.

Joni Eareckson, the quadriplegic young woman whose remarkable story has been written in two books, *Joni,* and *A Step Further,* is not old in years, but the seeming tragedy of a broken neck has made her old in spiritual maturity. She writes:

> If God had told me some time ago that He was about to make me as happy as I could be in this world, and then told me that He should begin by crippling arm or limb, and removing from me all my usual sources of enjoyment, I should have thought it a very strange way of accomplishing His purpose.
>
> And yet, how is His wisdom manifest in this? For if you should see a man shut up in a closed room, idolizing a set of lamps and rejoicing in their light, and you wished to make him truly happy, you would begin by blowing out his lamps, and then throw open the shutters to let in the light of heaven.[5]

Accepting the adverse factors of old age is the necessary preliminary to triumphing over them, and of discovering the new and exciting areas of fulfillment that only the passage of years can make possible.

THE AGING PROCESS

The transition from middle age to old age is thought by many to be one of the most testing periods of life. But there is an optimistic side even to that prognosis. These very tests offer the maturing Christian great opportunities for further development of Christian character. There are so many new situations and emergencies to be coped with and triumphed over. Our very rebellion against weakness and failing powers can be transmuted into spiritual attainment.

Many stupendous achievements have been chalked up by old and severely-handicapped people. Milton in the field of literature and Beethoven in music made their handicaps tributary to greater heights of success. Those men would not be daunted by their physical disabilities, nor did they allow their physical disabilities to determine their psychological age.

Milton wrote some of his finest poetry during his last twenty years, when he was completely blind. Beethoven composed some of his most glorious music toward the end of his life when he was completely deaf. How much poorer the world would have been without *Paradise Lost* and the Ninth Symphony.[6]

Many courageous elderly people, while accepting the inevitable frustrations of old age, regard these as challenges rather than as handicaps. They live according to their physiological, rather than their calendar age, and transcend their own problems by becoming absorbed in the needs of others.

Those who retain alertness and vitality into old age are not the ones who pamper and spare themselves, but those who live active and disciplined lives. That famous trio, the Misses Cable and French, who traversed the inhospitable Gobi Desert and suffered great hardships in the process, in their advancing years made visits to several home countries. They always declined to sit in soft, comfortable chairs when meetings were held in private homes. It was not that they were ascetics, but they were anticipating further service in the rugged Gobi, and would permit themselves nothing that would have a softening effect, and thus render them less effective in their divinely appointed task. They were effective to the end and each lived to a ripe age. It is inactivity, not activity, that depletes vitality.

NOTES

1. Henry Durbanville, *The Best Is Yet to Be* (Edinburgh: B. McCall Barbour, 1950), p. 12.
2. Ibid., p. 50.
3. Olive Wyon, *Emma Piechynska* (London: Hodder & Stoughton).
4. Paul Tournier, *Learning to Grow Old* (London: SCM, 1972), p. 169.
5. Joni Eareckson, *A Step Further* (Melbourne: S. John Bacon, 1978), p. 179.
6. Alfons Deeken, *Growing Old* (New York: Paulist, 1972), p. 9.

7

Retirement, A New Beginning

The word "retirement," with its understood promise of unlimited leisure, holds a world of allurement for some. Others approach it with dread and dismay, for they cannot imagine how they will be able to fill in all the extra time that was formerly occupied by their work.

Since retirement in one form or another comes to everyone sooner or later, it is not wisdom to ignore the fact and pretend it is not there. The prospect should be faced squarely and early, and plans set in motion to make it enjoyable, useful, and fulfilling. The inner attitude we adopt in facing what is undoubtedly a great crisis will determine in large measure the nature and quality of our retirement years.

There is an aura of finality about retirement that sometimes produces a state of shock. The process of aging is gradual, but retirement does not come on one gradually. Yesterday you were a worker. Today, for good or ill, you are a retired person. In current world conditions, workers have little choice in the matter. Redundancy often makes the unwelcome decision for them. There are few indeed for whom the experience does not create some degree of emotional upheaval.

An examination of retirement statistics yields somes interesting revelations. The British Ministry of Pensions reported that 60 percent of workers would like to continue working after retiring age. Seventy percent were still at work at sixty-five; 60 percent at seventy; 45 percent at seventy-five; and 66 percent of professional workers continue at work after sixty-five.

That clearly indicates that, either from choice or from necessity, the majority would rather continue working after reaching sixty-five than go into retirement. A Duke University study revealed that 55 percent of wives in the United States are sorry when their husbands have to retire. In the USA more than 25 percent of those over sixty-five work part or full-time from necessity.

Certain accompaniments of retirement tend to make it a traumatic experience. It usually involves loss of social status, and with that comes some loss of self-esteem and sense of worth. The compulsory surrender of accustomed authority, and forfeiture of the respect that goes with it, is keenly felt. Someone else now gives the orders!

Retirement is indeed a watershed that signals the unwelcome approach of old age. One is likely to feel significantly older the day after he retires—even though the only change is in the realm of employment. The essential person is just the same.

The fact that professional life is over means that a man almost inevitably feels that his expertise, purchased so dearly, is being wasted, and creative opportunities are at an end.

Another consequence is a decreasing interaction with society, and that often leaves the individual without any worthwhile goal, and with a sense of uselessness. The cheerful and friendly chatter that accompanies daily work can be sorely missed.

When children leave the family roof, it can be for the mother a close equivalent of retirement, in its emotional impact. The home suddenly seems so empty. After her busy life, there now seems less point in her existence, and motivation is lacking.

In cases where a couple have been so unwise as to build their lives and projected retirement around their family, the crisis will be exceptionally acute if the children move away. In this volatile world, separation of the members of a family is an increasing likelihood. Many years ago, when their children were young, two friends said to me that they did not intend to plan their retirement lives around their children because there were too many variables. As it happened, their children remained nearby, but it was wise forethought.

Those whose whole interest has centered on their daily work are likely to find retirement most traumatic. "Among men, the one to die is the one who has nothing but his job," writes Paul Tournier.[1] The person who during working years has cultivated the widest interests is the one who will best survive the shock of retirement.

Retirement can spawn a crop of fears which, if not promptly and resolutely dealt with, may shadow the closing years. They may include the fear of being unable to live on a reduced income; the fear of loneliness through being cut off from accustomed valued contacts; the fear of increasing disability, with a consequent sense of uselessness; fear of inability to profitably fill in the greatly increased leisure hours; fear of loss of mobility, and of being unable to afford to run a car. Especially difficult is the fear of not having one's driving license renewed, which has been described as one of the greatest indignities.

Those are all very real and painful phobias, but Paul assures us that "God hath not given us the spirit of fear, but of power and of love and of a sound mind" (2 Timothy 1:7, KJV). Perfect love casts out the fear that has torment (1 John 4:18). When fears assail us we can draw upon the divine assurance:

> He Himself has said. "I will never desert
> you, nor will I ever forsake you," so that
> we may confidently say, *"The Lord is my Helper,*
> *I will not be afraid.* What shall man do to me?"
> (Hebrews 13:5, italics added)

NEGATIVE OR POSITIVE?

Full enjoyment of old age for the retired person, will hinge on whether his approach is negative or positive. One attitude that can be adopted is to resist retirement for as long as possible, and then when it becomes inevitable, to resent it. When it is in his power, this type of person will hang on to his job and refuse to retire, even after his ability to cope has seriously waned; and in the process he will probably become increasingly authoritarian and unpopular. Christian work has suffered greatly at the hands of good men and women who have refused to retire long after their usefulness has declined, and have thus negated much valuable work. Their attitude only postpones the crisis, and in the meantime clouds life both for the older person and for others. As we grow older, we are not safe judges of the effectiveness or acceptability of our service.

The other attitude is to regard the retirement years as divinely-given opportunity for new adventure and achievement; to approach them not as an end, but as an exciting new beginning.

> While closing days leave something left to do,
> some deeper truth to learn, some gift to gain,
> Let me with cheerful mind my task pursue,
> And thankful, glean the fragments that remain.
>   T.D. Bernard

On the positive side, retirement can bring unexpected and rewarding opportunities to those who are alert to improve them. To the unexpectant, they will be few, but for the enthusiastic soul, exciting opportunities of service will not be lacking. They may be in another area of life, but that will only add zest and interest.

The limitations inherent in the aging process are largely in the area of physical activity rather than of the mind. The emphasis may now shift from *doing* to *being,* but is the latter less important than the former? That emphasis is not always welcomed by those who are by nature active.

It is noteworthy that whereas the active side of living receives prominence in the New Testament, even greater stress is laid on its passive aspects, that is, on *becoming,* not only on *doing.*

The beatitudes of Matthew 5:1-8 are largely passive in nature. The same is true, in the main, of the qualities of love enumerated in 1 Corinthians 13. The manifestations of the fruit of the Spirit in Galatians 5:22-23 are mainly passive, and each of them can flourish in the life of a person paralyzed from the neck down, unable to move a muscle. Does that have something to say to us?

Old age provides excellent soil in which the Holy Spirit can produce those attractive graces, and thus prepare us for heaven, while making us more pleasant to live with on earth. In this realm there is still the possibility of endless growth.

"The influence of a Christian in old age is one of cumulative and peculiar power," says an old writer. "It gathers into itself the forces of long-tried character, and is rich in ripened experience. The work which a Christian does in the closing years of life often has a spiritual vitality in it which busier earlier years had not."[2] True, he may have to abdicate the seat of power, but in exchange he can ascend the throne of wisdom.

It is important to learn early, preferably long before retirement, how to redirect the current of life into new channels of interest and activity so that retirement will not catch us unprepared. There will still be room for ambition, but it may require redirection into other avenues. Paul's driving ambition did not wane with the passing years. The danger for those who during working life had few subsidiary interests, is that they may lapse into inactivity and idleness. That must be guarded against at all costs.

RETIREMENT OCCUPATIONS

Retirement occupations and opportunities are many. There will be time to indulge and enjoy cherished hobbies begun in earlier years, or some new skill may be developed and put to constructive use. There will also be time for planned recreation and games.

A friend who enjoys working with wood has equipped a small workshop with lathe and other appropriate tools. Not only does he find relaxation and enjoyment in developing his own skill, but he invites youths from his church to his home, and gives them regular instruction in woodwork. That affords him a useful community service and also a chance to witness in a natural and congenial atmosphere.

Another friend, who is gifted artistically, conducts free classes in art, during which devotions are held. That gives friendly contact with many who would not come to church, as well as giving them valuable instruction.

For lovers of music, retirement is a bonanza and gives endless opportunities of developing musical appreciation or for exercising that gift. Although age may somewhat limit active participation, many old people can still perform very creditably. When in America recently, I visited a retirement home to see a lady of more than ninety years of age. She entertained me to two pieces of classical music played by memory, and with real skill. She has never stopped her regular practice.

Gardening is an ideal retirement occupation that can be most enjoyable and profitable. Many who have not had the opportunity of gardening in earlier life are diffident about making a beginning, and think they would not enjoy it. My advice would be ''give it a go,'' and you will find it a fascinating activity. It is eminently suited to the older person. It is a flexible pastime that can be adapted to one's physical capability. It can be gentle or vigorous according to taste.

Those who are not physically able to engage in strenuous horticultural pursuits could have a green house that would afford them perennial interest. The tending and cultivating of indoor potted plants will beautify the home, and give oneself and others continual pleasure.

In these days of rising prices, apart from the economic aspects, few things are more rewarding and even exciting than to make vegetables and flowers and shrubs grow. Dwarf fruit trees or trees grown espalier fashion are easily tended and produce surprisingly good crops. Then, too, gardening has the advantage of getting us out into the fresh air and sunshine.

For others, retirement years offer the longed-for chance to advance their education. Intellectual activity can enrich physical repose. An increasing number of older people, especially married women whose families are off their hands, are undertaking many of the courses of study that are available today. Capacity for intellectual pursuits continues long after physical vigor wanes. Classes for needlework and other such crafts are readily available.

Continuing Mental Growth

It is widely accepted that as long as disease does not impair our faculties, mental activity can continue increasing in old age.

At the age of eighty-one, Arnold Toynbee, the world-famous historian wrote:

> As one grows older, the temptation to dwell on the past and to avert one's eyes from the future, grows. If one were to fall into this backward-looking stance, one would be as good (I mean as bad) as dead before physical death had overtaken us . . . *Our minds, so long as they keep their cutting edge, are not bound by physical limits;* they can range over time and space into infinity. To be human is to be capable of transcending oneself.[3]

In the same strain, Pearl S. Buck, the noted authoress of eighty-four books, wrote in her eightieth year:

> Young and old for me are meaningless words except as we use them to denote where we are in this stage of being. Would I wish to be ''young again''? No, for I have learned too much to wish to lose it. It could be like failing to pass a good grade at school.
>
> I have reached an honourable position in life because I am old and no longer young. I am a far more useful person than I was fifty years ago, or forty years ago, or thirty, twenty, or even ten. *I have learned so much since I was seventy.*[4]

It is granted that those were unusually gifted people, but they have a message for us ordinary mortals that we should heed and act upon. The more the mind is exercised, the more enjoyable it is to exercise it.

The more one learns, the easier it is to learn. "Used brains usually last longer." When the mind slumps, the body tends to slump, and that happens most frequently when we lose our zest for the discovery of new and mind-stretching truths. The Christian who has consistently studied the Scriptures and relevant literature is in a very advantageous position in this respect.

Carl Jung, the noted psychologist, maintained that man worked and lived with only one half of his psychic capability while the other half remained unused and forgotten.

Reading is another rich and rewarding possibility. In the busier working years, it was easy for those who were not avid readers to neglect serious reading. But retirement opens up a new era of possibility. With the well-equipped public libraries that are available to all, the joy of reading can enable us to explore new and fascinating worlds. Selected reading provides one with a window on the whole world. Even though that exercise may have been neglected earlier, a firm purpose will soon develop an appetite for the rich literature available to the English-speaking public.

With increased leisure time comes the priceless opportunity of leisurely but systematic study of the sacred Scriptures. Have we not often, when faced with spiritual or theological problems, wished that we knew the Bible better? Now the possibility is right at our doors. There are numerous Bible correspondence courses that can be studied at our own pace, with the guidance of experienced instructors. And there are many very helpful Bible study books that we can follow for ourselves. However, the discipline of having tests to answer makes the correspondence course a valuable method to follow.

There are community services to be engaged in, such as "Meals on Wheels." Hospital visitation is a much appreciated, though somewhat neglected, ministry in which the sympathetic and understanding person will find abundant opportunity for loving community service. People in retirement homes also welcome some break in their routines, for many have few to visit them.

In the church, there are a wide variety of services an aging person can undertake. If an offer of service is made to the pastor, it will be unusual if there is no small but useful task he can suggest. Much can be done to alleviate the loneliness of "shut-ins," and small services such as mowing the lawn or helping with the heavier housework will be much appreciated.

ENJOYING LEISURE

With the rapid advances of automation in our time comes the prospect of a considerable reduction in working hours. That has the inevitable result of increasing leisure time. In the midst of the pressures of daily life, nothing seems more attractive. In the event, however, increased leisure can create new and unexpected problems.

Leisure has been defined as the state of having time at one's disposal; the opportunity afforded by unoccupied time. The key problem is how to employ that unoccupied time enjoyably and yet profitably. Often there is no simple answer, and it is a problem that must be worked at.

If the projections of some sociologists are to be taken seriously, and if technological advances make them possible, that possibility should be faced long before retirement.

Denis de Rougemont, director of the European Cultural Center, for example, made this almost incredible forecast: "In twenty or thirty years according to some experts, it will only be necessary for one third of the (greatly increased) population of the earth, to work for four hours a week, in order to satisfy all our 'material' needs (and much more adequately than is the case today)."[5]

For someone who even during his working life finds it difficult to fill leisure hours satisfyingly, such a prospect, far from being alluring, would be daunting and forbidding.

If we regard leisure as the converse of work, or as idleness, then it would indeed be disastrous and soul-destroying. That is already being experienced by many retired people. In spite of its many desirable and valuable features, the welfare state is creating a generation that demands support by the State as an inalienable right. The incentive to "do it yourself" is being eroded, and laziness is becoming endemic.

Leisure, however, is not to be equated with idleness enjoyed at the expense of others. Neither is it unoccupied time to be devoted to discovering ways in which one can avoid becoming bored. Leisure is time to be enjoyed and used in a manner that will be satisfying, and yet will make some contribution to society and to the kingdom of God.

On retirement, people use their leisure in a variety of ways such as travel, pursuing some hobby, sport, artistic pursuits, and so forth. But even those can produce boredom if there is no worthy end in view. It is essential to discover meaning and purpose, even in leisure. When daily work no longer provides motivation, another incentive and goal must be substituted — and for the Christian that will necessarily include some worthwhile contribution to the ongoing work of the kingdom of God.

If we are really to enjoy growing old, ideally we should begin preparing for retirement years early, and not leave it until old age is upon us. But few are fortunate in having attained that ideal, myself included. That does not mean that we can do nothing about it. Delay in tackling it only compounds the problem.

In order to give meaning and purpose to leisure hours, our pursuits or hobbies will need to be more than aimless time-killing. However, leisure, in order to be true leisure, should include the right to do what one likes without having a bad conscience about it. Leisure should give pleasure. The person who in his former life has been a "work-aholic" will not find it easy to achieve this state of mind in a hurry. Habit dies hard.

"Retired people still retain something of a feeling of guilt about leisure, even though they no longer have a duty to work at their jobs," said one sociologist. They must learn what may be for them a difficult lesson, that within limits, leisure is just as legitimate as work. In order to be enjoyed, leisure should not be regarded as time stolen from more important activity.

Any form of constructive work is a beneficial therapeutic activity, and as such should be valued and practiced. Contrary to the opinion of some, work is not a hardship to be avoided wherever possible, but an activity that will benefit both the individual and the community.

To employ leisure profitably will probably involve taking up new interests, being open to new ideas, making new friends. For the Christian, leisure affords a much longer time for the daily culture of the spiritual life, and that opportunity should be seized eagerly. There will be increased time to devote to Christian service that was not possible in working years. It may well be that the areas of service open to the elderly will afford less prominence and involve less physical activity, but that by no means implies that it will be less influential in the Lord's eyes, or make a less significant contribution to His kingdom.

NOTES

1. Paul Tournier, *Learning to Grow Old* (London: SCM, 1972), p. 162.
2. Henry Durbanville, *The Best Is Yet to Be* (Edinburgh: B. McCall Barbour, 1950), p. 46.
3. Arnold J. Toynbee, *Experiences* (London: Oxford U., 1969). Cited in Morton Puner, *To the Good, Long Life* (London: Macmillan, 1974), p. 275.
4. Puner, p. 273.
5. Denis De Rougemont, *Man's Western Quest* (London: Allen & Unwin, 1958), p. 4.

8

Not Too Late!

"God is not exclusively youth-oriented." This intriguing assertion is no more than the truth, although the program of some
churches would incline one to think He is! We older people need to
be reminded of that, for we tend to forget that God has an ideal plan
for the life of each old person, just as much as for each young
person. Age is immaterial to a God who knows no time as we
measure it. His personal interest in our welfare does not wane with
the passing years.

When we were younger, most of us who are Christians earnestly
sought to discover God's plan for our lives, especially when we
came to the crossroads of career and marriage. Are we equally
diligent in seeking His plan for our old age, or are we just drifting
along with no definite aim or goal?

With more time to review the past, it is not difficult to become
discouraged as we recall opportunities missed; a lessening of zeal in
God's service; a mediocre prayer life; or perhaps actual sins of
which we have reason to be ashamed. It is at such moments of
introspection that we need to turn our eyes outward and upward to
our loving and understanding Father. What balm a verse like Romans 5:20 can bring! "But where sin increased, grace abounded all
the more."

The wonderful thing about God's abundant grace and favor is that
it is never too late to discover and follow God's plan for the remain-
der of our lives, never too late to make a new start, even if we have
missed His plan up till the present time.

To his discouraged and disillusioned compatriots, the prophet Joel
brought an inspiring message of hope—the hope of a new beginning. God delights in giving His failing children a chance to begin
again. Here, in part, was His message to those disheartened old men:

61

Hear this, O elders, . . . Has anything like this happened in your days or in your fathers' days? . . . What the gnawing locust has left, the swarming locust has eaten; and what the swarming locust has left, the creeping locust has eaten; and what the creeping locust has left, the stripping locust has eaten [Joel 1:2-4].

So rejoice, O sons of Zion, and be glad in the LORD your God . . . Then I will make up to you for the years that the swarming locust has eaten, the creeping locust, the stripping locust and the gnawing locust, My great army which I sent among you. And you shall have plenty to eat and be satisfied, and praise the name of the LORD your God, Who has dealt wondrously with you . . . Thus you will know that I am in the midst of Israel, and that I am the LORD your God" [Joel 2:23-27].

LOST YEARS RESTORED

What new hope and optimistic expectations this divine undertaking would kindle in the hearts of the old men. *"I will restore"* the locust-eaten years is the RSV translation (Joel 2:25). And who of us has had no locust-eaten years — years that have been barren of truly fruitful worship and service? We can take heart; *the best is yet to be!* It is not too late.

The promise thus made to Israel was of a restoration of material prosperity. Is there biblical warrant for appropriating that promise to ourselves in a spiritual sense? Indeed there is. God promised Abraham that his seed would be ''as the sand which is on the seashore'' — his earthly offspring — and ''as the stars of the heavens'' — his heavenly seed (Genesis 22:17). Abraham's earthly seed, the Jewish nation, were heirs to the *material blessings* promised by God. Paul explains our part in it: ''And if you belong to Christ, then you are Abraham's offspring, heirs according to the promise'' (Galatians 3:29). As his spiritual offspring, we are entitled to claim the *spiritual blessings* implied in the promise. That is the way Peter treated this very passage on the day of Pentecost (Acts 2:16-21).

The locust can assume many forms — opportunities given but not utilized, time spent on matters of secondary importance, unworthy motivation, words that have been idle or wounding, sins that have not been mortified. Have some of those ''locusts'' robbed our lives of the freshness and greenness of our earlier Christian experience, as well as robbing God of the harvest due to Him?

To us failing men and women, the Holy Spirit whispers, "I will restore *to you* the years that the locust has eaten."

"But," you may protest, "I have always been told that time lost can never be recovered! That opportunities missed are gone forever!" But here is a promise of God that bypasses time. The things impossible to man are possible with God.

When traveling in the southern part of Taiwan, I was shown lush and verdant rice fields. The farmer told me that a few years previously, he was able to produce only one crop of rice a year. But with the aid of technologists, fertilizer, and better seed supplied through American aid projects, he could now produce three crops of rice in a year from the same land.

It is gloriously possible to make up for lost time! As with the Taiwanese farmer, God can give us three spiritual harvest in the one year. Is that not one way in which we can make up for lost time and opportunity? The past cannot be recalled, but this evangel of hope assures us that upon confession there is full and free forgiveness for *all past sin,* through the powerful blood of Christ (1 John 1:9). No past failure makes future victory less possible. Indeed, God can cause our very failure to contribute to our victorious living by producing humility and brokenness and a deeper dependence on Him.

A SECOND CHANCE

Nature offers us no second chance if we infringe her laws. Nor do our fellowmen, very often. But our God not only forgives our sin and forgets our past, but He offers us a *new opportunity, a second chance.* Was that not true of Jonah, Jacob, David, Peter, John Mark, and a host of others? It is not too late for us to begin again. Hear the Lord's word to us all:

> *"Yet even now,"* declares the LORD, "Return to Me with all your heart, and with fasting, weeping and mourning; and rend your hearts and not your garments." Now return to the LORD your God, for He is gracious and compassionate, slow to anger, abounding in lovingkindness, and relenting of evil" [Joel 2:12-13, italics added].

In my youth we used to sing a sacred song entitled *The Bird with the Broken Wing,* by Hezekiah Butterworth. It ended with the doleful lines:

> But the bird with the broken pinion,
> Never soared as high again.

The message of the song was obviously intended to be that for the wounded bird, whose very life depended on its wing, only a life of limitation and frustration lay ahead. The possibility of soaring into the blue was gone forever.

The words of the song were set to music by Peter Bilhorn, a popular American singing evangelist. On one occasion he sang it in the Iowa state prison.

When he concluded the song, one of the convicts rose and said, "Chaplain, is that true? If what he has been singing is true, there is no hope for me, or for a lot of us here." He resumed his seat with a sob.

Peter Bilhorn realized the validity of the man's deeply felt protest, but it was too late to explain. He returned to his home saying to himself, "It's not true!" Did Scripture not say, "Where sin increased, grace abounded all the more" (Romans 5:20)? A few days later he added two verses to the song to correct the error.

> But the soul that comes to Jesus
>   Is saved from every sin,
> And the heart that fully trusts Him
>   Shall a crown of glory win.
>
> Then come to the dear Redeemer,
>   He will cleanse you from every stain,
> By the grace that He freely gives you,
>   *You shall soar as high again.*

That was not the end of the story. Almost twenty years later, a colonel approached Mr. Bilhorn at a YMCA gathering.

"You don't remember me, but I remember you," he said. "You visited Fort Madison prison eighteen years ago, and sang about a bird with a broken wing. I am the man who asked you if it was true. When you came again and sang the added verses, I gave my heart to

Christ, and was able to rise. By God's grace one can 'higher soar again.' "[1]

A VESSEL UNTO HONOR

The familiar parable of the potter (Jeremiah 18:1-6) illustrates the same optimistic possibility. Although we may be advanced in years, the heavenly Potter has not yet put the finishing touches to our lives. There are still glorious possibilities ahead. The past was not better than the future can yet be.

When the beautiful ornament the potter was fashioning of clay collapsed under his hand, he might well have thrown the recalcitrant clay on the scrap-heap, and taken a fresh lump that would be more responsive to his molding touch. But he did not do so. Instead, "he remade it into another vessel, as it pleased the potter to make" (Jeremiah 18:4). Even when we have thwarted the purpose of the divine Potter in our lives, He does not despair of us and cast us aside, as Satan, "the accuser of the brethren" (Job 1:6) would have us believe. We can still pray,

> Make use of me my God,
> Let me not be forgot,
> A broken vessel cast aside,
> One whom Thou usest not.
>
> All things do serve Thee here,
> All creatures great and small,
> Make use of me, of me my God,
> The meanest of them all.
>
> H. Bonar

The reworked vessel may not be as beautiful as the one the heavenly Potter originally planned, but it can still become "a vessel for honor, sanctified, useful for the Master, prepared for every good work" (2 Timothy 2:21). The divine Potter is undiscourageable.

In one of his choice sermons on the parable of the potter, J. Stuart Holden concluded with this peroration:

> The last appeal to the marred vessel is the marred face. He was a marred vessel, marred by sin not his own, but mine and yours. I pray, ere we separate, look into His marred face, and see there the power for the remaking of the marred vessel.

From "Morituri Salutamus"

It is too late! Ah, nothing is too late
Till the tired heart shall cease to palpitate.
Cato learned Greek at eighty; Sophocles
Wrote his grand Œdipus, and Simonides
Bore off the prize of verse from his compeers
When each had numbered more than fourscore years;
And Theophrastus, at fourscore and ten,
Had but begun his "Characters of Men."

Chaucer, at Woodstock, with the nightingales,
At sixty wrote the Canterbury Tales.
Goethe at Weimar, toiling to the last,
Completed Faust when eighty years were past.
. . . .
What then? Shall we sit idly down and say
The night hath come; it is no longer day?
. . . .
For age is opportunity no less
Than youth itself, though in another dress.
And as the evening twilight fades away
The sky is filled with stars, invisible by day.

H. W. Longfellow

NOTES

1. Henry Durbanville, *The Best Is Yet to Be* (Edinburgh: B. McCall Barbour, 1950), pp. 16-18.

9

No Pipe Dream

The possibility of another career after retirement is by no means a mere pipe dream. Retirement can open the door to new and exciting experiences. My successor as general director of the Overseas Missionary Fellowship, Michael Griffiths, after serving eleven years in that office, has now begun another career as principal of the London Bible College. His present career may well prove to be more influential than his previous ones.

Because retirement has come, one need not feel that his maximum contribution to the kingdom of God lies in the past. It is both foolish and unwarranted to act as though effective working days were ended. Between disengagement and disability there can be a most fruitful period, suited to one's age. It may be a less active career, and yet even more influential.

Longfellow recognized this possibility:

> For age is opportunity no less
> Than youth itself, though in another dress.
> And as the evening twilight fades away,
> The sky is filled with stars, invisible by day.

This has been my own experience. When I was seventy years old, I received a telephone call from a friend in Australia saying they were having difficulty in finding a principal for the Christian Leaders' Training College in Papua New Guinea, and inquiring if I might be available for the task. As my wife had only recently been called home, I was without home ties, and gladly welcomed the prospect of a demanding new assignment at that poignant time.

It was a multifaceted work in a setting entirely different from previous experience, but it proved richly rewarding. It was a great privilege at that stage of life to have a part in the molding of the lives of a fine body of young New Guinean Christian leaders. As a most appreciated bonus, I had the joy of ministering the Word to almost a score of conferences of missionaries and national leaders in various parts of Papua New Guinea. That experience was no pipe dream.

Another career can be commenced at any time, but to make it a success will demand strong motivation and much determination. A second career or a third career is often differently motivated from the first—for it is freely chosen, and there is usually no element of necessity. Sheer love of it is more likely to be the motive than cold duty. It will bring the blessedness of which Alexander Pope wrote when he said, "Blessed is he who has found his work. And let him ask no further blessedness."

Such a new career could be found in the area of voluntary Christian or humanitarian work, opportunities for which should not be difficult to find. Those who are skilled in certain arts or crafts can find new avenues in which to exploit their gifts. The gardener can raise plants or grow flowers to sell or to brighten the homes of shut-ins. Or he can experience the thrill of developing new strains of plants. Likewise, the amateur photographer will find many avenues of service to others. Those with literary inclinations now have abundant time to exercise and develop their gift. The skilled typist will never be out of work.

To a degree not possible in the past, elderly people in good health can find rewarding avenues of service on some mission fields. One lady known to me went to Brazil at the age of seventy and did missionary work for three years. She then went to Papua New Guinea and did much appreciated work there until she was eighty. Of course such cases may be regarded as exceptional, but they are the exceptions that prove the rule.

Abraham is a luminous biblical example of a man who began a second, exciting career at the age of seventy-five. He was no callow youth thirsting for adventure when the disturbing challenge came to him: "Go forth from your country, and from your relatives and from your father's house, to the land which I will show you" (Genesis 12:1). It says much for his obedience and that of his wife (she was only ten years younger) that "by faith Abraham, when he was called, obeyed by going out . . . not knowing where he was going" (Hebrews 11:8).

It must have been a traumatic experience for Sarah to break up her luxurious home — for Ur was a highly civilized city and her husband was a wealthy man. To leave her treasures behind and take only such things as would be appropriate for a nomadic life must have involved a great wrench. For comfortable city-dwellers to change their whole life-style and sacrifice their security at that time of life required faith and courage of a more than ordinary degree.

But God disturbs at will, and at any time of life. He does not ask us if it is convenient, and as was the case with Abraham, He does not always offer a speedy explanation. He expects to be trusted. Scripture tells us that it was "by faith" that Abraham and Sarah effected the transition, and this first step led ultimately to his becoming known as "the father of the faithful." His obedience in his old age, though severely tested, brought blessing to the whole world. The promise was fulfilled: "In thee shall all families of the earth be blessed" (Genesis 12:3, KJV). Are we as ready to take a new step of faith should the Lord so indicate?

10

Paradox of Renewal

As with his Master, the sufferings and pressures of Paul's life made him old long before his time. When some of His enemies were arguing with Jesus, they cynically said to Him, "You are not yet fifty years old," when He was in fact only thirty (John 8:57). He had allowed sorrow to do its work in Him and it had left its mark. Paul too bore in his body the marks, the scars of his Lord (Galatians 6:17). When many of his own age were still in their prime, his persecutions and beatings had made him a prematurely old man. To gain some idea of the mounting crescendo of trials that beset him, take the time now to read: 2 Corinthians 1:8; 2:4; 4:8; 6:4-10; 7:5; 11:23-28; 12:7.

Small wonder he said that his "outer man" was wasting away (2 Corinthians 4:16). The "earthen vessel" of 2 Corinthians 4:7 was visibly crumbling. The pains and perils and pressures of his incredible missionary labors were gradually wearing him down.

But that was not the whole story, for while that disintegration was taking place, a counter-process was going on simultaneously.

> Therefore we do not lose heart, but though our outer nature is decaying, yet *our inner man is being renewed day by day* [2 Corinthians 4:16, italics added].

It almost seems as though Paul was a dispassionate onlooker, calmly watching the disintegration of his own body. Even though the process was being accelerated by the persecution of his enemies, that appeared to cause him little concern. He knew that at the same time his inner man was developing new graces and strengths every day.

Those very afflictions were the medium by which his Father was giving inner renewal, and thus fulfilling His gracious purposes. Paul

71

discovered that there was available a daily supply of spiritual power sufficient to equip him for the appointed service of each day. Have we learned that lesson?

In the life of the non-Christian, the disintegration of the outward nature is a melancholy sight, for there is no counter-process taking place. All is loss. But for the Christian, trial, tribulation, and even death itself cannot reach or affect adversely that inner life that is hid with Christ in God (Colossians 3:3). He is possessor of a life that is above and independent of circumstances.

"To wear life out in the service of Jesus is to open it to the entrance of Jesus' life [2 Corinthians 4:10]; it is to receive, in all its alleviations, in all its renewals, in all its deliverances, a witness to His resurrection."[1] Every day Paul received new accessions of strength from God.

There is no indication that he was the recipient of special favors not open to his fellow believers — or to us. We have all been equally blessed "with every spiritual blessing" (Ephesians 1:3). The obvious discrepancy between Paul's radiant experience and our own is explained by the fact that *every day* he constantly and actively appropriated and made his own his share in that divine provision, whereas too often we leave our equally available share unappropriated.

Though Paul must very often have been near the point of collapse — and our Father is not indifferent to the cost of our service — yet, because he daily drew on the supernatural strength of God, instead of collapsing, he experienced inner renewal.

He explains that secret renewal in a series of striking paradoxes:

> For momentary, light affliction is producing for us an eternal weight of glory far beyond all comparison, while we look not at the things which are seen, but at the things which are not seen; for the things which are seen are temporal, but the things that are not seen are eternal [2 Corinthians 4:17-18].

In this paradoxical process, God uses the very affliction that is causing the disintegration of his body to effect an inner renewal that lifts him far above the tyranny of the physical. In Paul's reckoning,

> The heavy burden is light.
> The ethereal glory is a weight.

The seemingly endless trials are momentary.
The transient afflictions bring eternal blessing.

It should be noted that that inner renewal takes place "while," (or "because," as it is in some translations) "we look not at the things which are seen" — the pressures, persecutions, daily dying that were his present lot — "but at the things which are not seen" — the glory of the Lord as seen in the face of Jesus Christ (2 Corinthians 4:18). The glory of Christ and the transforming power which was the fruit of His sufferings are eternal and unfading. The agent in the transformation is "the Lord, the Spirit" (2 Corinthians 3:18).

Paul would thus encourage us to believe that although old age erodes our bodily forces and we "waste away," and though the process may be hastened in the case of some who are exposed to more than ordinary trials, the same powerful inner renewal as he experienced can be ours *every day*. And it will be adequate to enable us to fulfill the divine plan for every day.

"No wonder we do not lose heart!" exclaimed Paul.

> Lord, it belongs not to my care
> Whether I die or live;
> To love and serve Thee is my share,
> And this thy grace must give.

> If life be long, I will be glad,
> That I may long obey;
> If short, yet why should I be sad
> That shall have the same pay?

Richard Baxter

NOTES

1. James Denney, "Second Corinthians," in *Expositor's Bible*, ed. W. Robertson Nicoll (Grand Rapids: Eerdmans, 1956), p. 757.

11

Disabilities Need Not Always Disable

Growing older is not a disease, nor is old age a synonym for disability, even though Seneca described old age as "an incurable disease."

Although that is true, it is both realistic and wise to recognize that in most cases, apart from the illnesses that are common to the whole community, elderly people can expect to suffer some of the other disabilities peculiar to their age bracket. But even so, there are no grounds for undue or universal pessimism. Some, of whom I fortunately am one, after having experienced disability in earlier life, are exceptionally blessed in being subject to few of those in later life. But those people are more the exception than the rule.

In the ordinary course of things, disabilities will increase, not diminish, although recent advances in medical science and treatment have done a great deal to improve the lot of the aged in this respect. Conditions that previously proved incurable can now be sucessfully treated.

There is a statistical likelihood that disabilities *caused by disease* will increase after we pass the sixty mark, although many disabilities are not caused by age but by an unhealthy environment. But there is some comfort in the findings of doctors who work in the geriatric field.

In old age, disease does not necessarily mean permanent disability. Many diseases, if treated early, are remediable even in the aged. Some diseases are amenable to self-cure where the will is present. The effects of most diseases can be ameliorated even if not cured, through the appropriate therapy and nursing skill.

Where there is medical evidence that a disability is likely to be permanent, it is wisdom for the sufferer to accept the inevitable courageously, and with good grace. To adopt any other course is to

75

lay oneself open to depression, frustration, and self-pity.

On the positive side, it is the experience of many that the two decades from sixty to eighty can be one of the most enjoyable and useful periods of life. Incapacity comes at no particular age, and can even be staved off through strength of purpose and a courageous attitude. Many conditions usually regarded as inevitable can be avoided.

It was my privilege recently to share a conference ministry with Dr. Herbert Lockyer, Sr. In spite of his ninety-two years, he delivered fine, God-blessed messages. Three books from his pen were published that year! His age and physical frailty had not greatly diminished his spiritual output.

In their solicitude for our welfare, our friends are often overly kind to us, and tend to be overprotective. They are apprehensive about our going out by ourselves as we become less mobile. "You shouldn't do that at your age," is an often-heard injunction. On the slightest pretext they kindly rush to help us. But it is not always healthy to wrap the elderly in cotton wool too early.

Wherever possible, a disabled person would be well-advised to do all he can for himself for as long as he can. Caring friends should allow him the opportunity of doing such things as are within his capacity for as long as possible. Overanxiety or overprotection on the part of loved ones can turn one who is partly disabled into an invalid. Their recovery may be retarded by that well-intentioned attitude.

By all means give every assistance to the infirm or disabled. But most of them would rather die in harness than lose their independence. So let them have it for as long as possible.

WHAT DID YOU SAY?

One of the more distressing limitations that comes with the passing years is a progressive loss of hearing; distressing, not so much for the limitation itself, inconvenient though it is, but because it creates a tendency to withdraw into oneself. The sufferer's world grows smaller and smaller, and that can produce a sense of acute isolation — a condition that can lead to psychological problems.

The fact must be faced realistically — some loss of sensitivity in hearing is a normal accompaniment of aging; but deafness is not a part of normal senescence. That is borne out by the fact that so many older people have quite acute hearing, as we soon discover if we speak as though they were not present! Our bodily senses do, however, become less acute with age. It is normal for older people to fail to hear high-pitched sounds, for example.

Deafness usually develops very gradually, and often almost unnoticed, until suddenly we find ourselves saying all too frequently, "I beg your pardon, what did you say?" I remember very clearly reaching that stage. Or we begin to notice that people seem to speak more quietly and indistinctly than they used to, and we cannot catch what they are saying. The tendency is at first to attribute the problem to the poor enunciation of those who speak to us. "I wish you wouldn't mutter at me," complained an elderly lady.

In point of fact, they were not muttering or speaking indistinctly, but her ability to hear and correctly interpret the sounds had unconsciously deteriorated. The root problem in many cases is not so much inability to hear, as a slowing-up of the ability to interpret and respond to what is heard. Again that is borne out by the embarrassing discovery that deaf people seem adept at hearing what they were not intended to hear. It is never safe to talk about deaf people as if they were not present.

Blindness creates an almost automatic sympathy for the sufferer tapping his way along the street, and a spontaneous desire to be helpful. But that is not so much the case with the equally handicapped deaf person. People are by no means as patient and sympathetic with them, partly because their disability is less easily recognized.

Though it does not arouse as much sympathy, loss of hearing is, if possible, an even greater handicap than blindness, and more disturbing to the aging person. The difficulty of communication deafness causes often produces more impatience and irritation than compassion, driving the subject into deeper isolation. Further, it tends to discourage the habit of listening. In extreme cases aging people give up the losing battle to hear. They may even pretend to be deafer than they are, so as to avoid being embarrassed or being laughed at for any faux pas their deafness may have caused.

It is not only the deaf who fail to hear. People who have normal hearing often fail to hear when addressed because they are preoccupied with something that is more important to them. Hearing depends in large measure on such a concentration of mind as blocks out other sounds. The aging person who is growing deaf will be liable to "turn off" when undesirable or irrelevant conversation is in progress. But he will immediately and automatically "turn on" again if there is a subject of personal interest. The same is true with singing. If the words are not clearly enunciated, the deaf person gives up the attempt to hear.

Sometimes friends attempt to compensate for the loss of hearing by shouting at the one they are addressing. That does not always achieve the desired end. The need is more for clarity and distinct enunciation than for turning up the volume.

With growing deafness, it is more difficult to hear well at a party or a group meeting, even when one is not too handicapped in face-to-face conversation. This is an almost inevitable development that many just have to learn to live with. It can, of course, be ameliorated if other people will take the trouble to draw the deaf person into the conversation and to speak directly and clearly to them. But deafness often produces a sensitivity about being a trouble to others.

There is a definite technique for speaking to a deaf person so as to aid their hearing, and the following technique has been found helpful:

> You should not begin speaking until you are face to face with the listener. Your face should preferably be in a good light and on the same level as the deaf person, so that he can supplement his hearing by observing your lips and expression. Speak slowly, and accentuate all consonants. It is helpful to use gestures. Speak slowly, but don't shout.

When hearing begins to fail, one of the most helpful aids is to learn lip-reading. Although one may not fully master this art, it can prove a most valuable help in audible communication. Many people develop such an extraordinary dexterity that one almost forgets that they are deaf.

If deafness develops rapidly, it would be wise to consult the doctor at once, for there may be some cause other than normal loss of hearing. The cheerful discovery may be made that the trouble is no more serious than an undue accumulation of wax, which can easily be syringed out!

There have been great advances in the field of hearing aids, and although they may not offer a complete remedy, they can be of great assistance in certain forms of deafness. Hearing aids should be adopted earlier rather than later. Many who have tried them only when well advanced in years have been disappointed because they have been unable to adapt to them. The fact that *all* sounds are amplified, and not only what one is anxious to hear, can result in confusion, and results in little alleviation of the deafness when several people in a group are speaking. Here as elsewhere, it is practice that makes perfect. Many give up the attempt to master the hearing aid too soon, and thus lose the very real assistance they can give.

MEMORY PLAYING TRICKS?

With advancing age, it cannot be denied that some degree of impairment of our powers of memory is a distinct possibility, but that is by no means inevitable. Far too many old people have excellent memories to justify such an unqualified assertion. Mild memory failure may be normal. From middle age onward a slow decline in the ability to quickly recall the names of people and places is not uncommon. Especially when one is overtired or tense, the memory of recent events may be less sharp. But although some memory loss is a sign of aging it is not an essential characteristic of being old.

Samuel Chadwick, a noted Methodist preacher of the earlier days of the century, wrote a whimsical editorial in his paper *Joyful News* (17 September 1931). In the article he made reference to his problem with his memory as he approached old age:

> Memory plays some queer tricks these days. I never had a good verbal memory, and I have always been thankful for a word of comfort spoken to me by an aged minister, Rev. Joshua Priestley, when I was a lad.
>
> He told me not to be discouraged, for a good memory was by no means the best gift, and might easily become a snare. I have lived to agree with him, but I find a tricky memory a great trial. I have had what I might call a good index memory. If I could not recite, I have known where to find what I wanted, even to the position on the page.
>
> People's names and faces I do not remember, but an incident or an argument I never forget. I can always work my way back to a person through some association, but my index memory has taken to playing

me tricks. The thing I want eludes me, and then when I am not seeking I find. The thing I want pops out and says Boo!

I think many of us are able to identify with Mr. Chadwick in his experience. The widespread belief that memory inexorably declines with age, and recent memory more rapidly than the remote, is strongly challenged by some researchers. It has been found that those who have habitually exercised their memories retained them longest. Indeed, that is true of all our faculties.

Morton Puner, a member of the Gerontological Society in the USA, contends that there is no inexorable reason why our mental abilities, including memory, may not remain largely unchanged long after eighty, and that mental competence may — and should — improve with age. Memory need not have age limits at all, provided of course that ill health or other exceptional circumstances do not intervene.[1]

The tendency of the aging person to live a great deal in the past is not necessarily a mark of senility. For many, though by no means for all, the past has been much more pleasant than the present circumstances, and it is not surprising therefore, if memory reverts nostalgically to a happier past. Memory does happily cooperate in burying the painful and remembering the pleasant, and that can make the past seem much happier in retrospect than it really was in actual fact.

One cause of past events' being more clearly remembered than recent happenings could be the fact that aging people very often are no longer having experiences that make the present equally as significant as the past. Again, recent experiences may not have been registered on the memory so deeply and stored in its data bank.

I remember in my youth hearing Alexander Watson, the celebrated Shakesperian reciter, who knew and could recite all of Shakespeare's plays. He related that on one occasion he was called upon suddenly to substitute for an actor who had dropped out. He had to learn the play very quickly, and not nearly so thoroughly as was his usual custom. He managed to fill his part without mishap. With all the other plays he had memorized, once he had learned them, he never had to learn them again. But he had to relearn the play he had superficially memorized each time he played it. The initial impression on his mind was superficial and not deep. As we get older, it seems that events are not etched as deeply on our memories as was the case in our youth.

Memory can be tyrannical in recalling the failures and sins of the past. In what clear relief our subtle adversary, Satan, makes them stand out!

George Matheson, the blind poet and preacher, put into poignant words the yearning of many hearts so troubled.

> O to go back across the years long vanished,
> To have the words unsaid, the deeds undone;
> The errors cancelled, the deep shadows banished
> In the glad sense of a new world begun.
> To be a little child, whose page of story
> Is yet undimmed, unblotted by a stain;
> And in the sunrise of primeval glory
> To know that life has had its start again.

But there is a bright ray of hope!

> I may go back across the years long vanished,
> I may resume my childhood, Lord, in Thee,
> When in the shadow of Thy cross, is banished
> All other shadows that encompass me.
> And o'er the road that now is dark and dreary,
> This soul, made buoyant by the strength of rest,
> Shall walk untired, shall run and not be weary,
> To bear the blessing that has made it blest.

Paul's former bigotry and blasphemy, his sadistic persecution of the saints, and his hatred of the gospel were never completely erased from his memory. While confessing that he was the worst of sinners, he refused to allow his memory to tyrannize over him. The memory of his past sin kept him humble, but he did not allow it to paralyze him for present service. "Forgetting what lies behind, and reaching forward . . . " (Philippians 3:13) was his consistent attitude, and it should be ours too. Paul used his past tragic failures as "a launching-pad for new heights of spiritual attainment."

> Man can forgive, and yet doth oft remember
> The past transgression; but God's heart so tender
> Doth cast our sins into the deepest sea,
> Nor e'er brings back cleansed guilt to memory.
>
> Author Unknown

Once we have mastered the lessons our failures have taught us, we should resolutely banish them from our memories. The advice of an old saint is well worth following: "Waste no tears upon the blotted record of past years, but turn the leaves and smile to see the fair white pages that remain to thee."

Looking backward can be of great value when, as with the oarsman, the backward look serves to give the impetus, and gain the momentum to go forward at greater speed. Looking back is valid when it moves us to aggressive action rather than complacent nostalgia.

Loss of memory may in some cases be voluntary. When old people become disoriented and lose contact with the outside world, they sometimes "allow their minds to go, to protect themselves from the sad knowledge that they are alone."[2] That the memory loss is voluntary, although subconscious at times, is evidenced by the fact that in some cases, when they are once again made to feel that they are loved and wanted, memory returns.

AN OPTIMISTIC VIEWPOINT

Some elderly Christians are distressed because they are unable to retain or recall what they read in their devotions. They chide themselves, as if it were something culpable on their part. One troubled lady mourned, "I can't even recall the promises of Scripture!"

That is indeed regrettable, but not culpable; nor is it irremediable. My father used to carry around little notebooks in which he had jotted choice portions of Scripture or helpful thoughts on which he could meditate. Why not adopt that aid to a failing memory?

An aged friend provided me with one of the most optimistic examples of how to enjoy growing old in spite of a faulty memory. He had been a diligent Bible student and teacher all his life, but now his memory was failing, and he could no longer recall what he had read and studied.

"I read a passage in the morning," he said, "and all kinds of new thoughts come into my mind. I think, 'I have never seen that truth before!' Of course I know I have read it hundreds of times before, and probably preached on it, but it comes to me now as fresh as if it was the first time I had read it." What a wholesome outlook! Rejoice in the truth of the Scripture and promises you are reading *while you read them,* even if you forget them afterward. They are still in the Bible, and you can turn to them again.

Make a prisoner on paper of promises or helpful thoughts you wish to remember. And take comfort in the fact that even if you forget the promises, *God does not forget them.*

> Look back and read life's passing story;
>   Has God e'er failed thee yet?
> Did not His presence go before thee?
>   His love canst thou forget?
> Remember all the past and trust Him only
>   For future days to be,
> If He is thine, thou canst no more be lonely,
>   He will be all to thee.

Fairlie Thornton

Notes

1. Morton Puner, *To the Good, Long Life* (London: Macmillan, 1974), p. 86.
2. William A. Nolen, "Senility and How You Can Avoid it," *McCalls,* October 1971.

12

A Major Preoccupation

Without doubt, and not without reason, the subject of health is a major preoccupation of the elderly. This is the field of the medical specialist, not of the layman. But as it impinges on the subject of aging at so many points, I venture, with due humility, to mention some areas of health — both physical and psychological — on which there appears to be a great deal of medical agreement.

Although all aging people must expect to encounter some of the disabilities peculiar to old age, ill health will not necessarily be the lot of all. Many worry excessively about their health, when they would probably enjoy better health if they largely ignored it. Of course serious illness is a different matter.

Old age and ill health do not automatically go together. Our hair does go gray, or disappears; we do get a little short of breath; our muscles do deteriorate somewhat, and our bodies slowly wear out. In spite of those inconveniences, however, robust health right into old age is enjoyed by many. The fact that even in old age some diseases respond so well to treatment is evidence that old age and illness are not synonymous.

It is a genuine anxiety of those of advanced age that they may fall ill and become a burden to friends and loved ones. That may indeed happen. The possibility must be faced, and whatever contingencies can reasonably be foreseen should be planned for.

Although we live in our bodies, they are strongly affected and influenced by our attitude of mind and the state of our emotions. Those react on each other, and both areas call for self-discipline if we are to enjoy general well-being. For example, if we neglect reasonable mental exercise or physical activity, the probable result will be apathy and boredom.

A great deal can be done today to eliminate or ameliorate many of the adverse effects that flow from disease. New drugs can greatly retard the progress of such illnesses as Parkinson's disease. In some cases the cure lies in our own hands. Obesity is one of the causes of ill health in old age. In most, though not all cases, it is the simple result of eating more food than the aging body needs or can assimilate.

As we grow older, the body burns up less fat in energy because we are less active than before. The remedy is obvious and simple to apply, but the motivation is often not sufficiently strong to move to action. The person involved may object that he is not a big eater. But that is not the point. The fact of increasing weight is sufficient evidence that more food than is required has been consumed, and that the intake of energy-generating foods is in excess of need.

That is something no one else can remedy for us. At the age of sixty-five it is generally held that one needs 20 percent less calories to maintain bodily functions than at twenty-five.

AREAS OF HEALTH CONCERN

Several areas of health are of special concern and apprehension to the elderly.

Blood-pressure is one of them. It is the part of wisdom to have regular medical checks, so that incipient trouble can be detected early. As our arteries narrow with age, a greater pressure is necessary to force the blood through them, and that is reflected in the higher figures recorded. Unless the reading is excessively high, there is no cause for alarm. Your doctor will advise you on this. Obesity can be a contributory cause of heightened blood-pressure.

Incontinence is often another secret dread, and this anxiety is equally shared by those on whom the responsibility for their care may devolve. This complaint, with its loss of independence, has been called the final humiliation. The prospect is especially distressing for those of very refined or fastidious natures, and to those who cherish a fierce independence.

But there is good news for many such anxious souls. Incontinence is by no means inevitable. In many cases it is not incurable and may prove to be only an episode, if treated in the early stages. It is important, however, that the root cause of the trouble be discovered and treated as speedily as possible.

Competent medical opinion affirms that even among people in their eighties, the number of those suffering from this distressing condition is not very great, and that many of those so affected can be successfully treated. Records show that in 1965 in Britain, 94 percent of those over sixty-five lived in their own homes, and only 1 percent were living in psychiatric hospitals. It was among the latter that the majority of the sufferers from incontinence were found.

One gerontologist has said that incontinence is generally comparatively rare and that the elderly person need not be preoccupied with the possibility of its occurring. Old age, of itself, does not lead to incontinence. It has been found in some cases that undue dependence on sleeping drugs has been a contributory cause.

A kindred problem is that of *bowel action*. With some, this becomes a major cause of concern. But for one who may experience a less than daily bowel action, there is good news too. Reliable medical opinion affirms that, although a daily bowel action may be desirable, it sometimes happens that a normal motion is achieved only every second or third day. This pattern does not necessarily cause any harm. Medical help may be needed in some cases, but self-prescription of strong laxatives is an unwise procedure. Medical advice should be secured where constipation is a real problem. The same is true when there is undue urinary frequency.

An increasingly common concomitant of old age is a *stroke,* which can result in loss of speech and partial paralysis. After the age of seventy about one person in ten is likely to suffer this disability in greater or lesser degree. It is indeed a distressing condition, but modern medical methods have in a growing number of cases greatly minimized its consequences, and many of us will know of friends who have recovered so fully as to be able to resume reasonably normal living and a great degree of activity.

Correct nutrition plays an important part in the maintenance of health in old age, and one helpful contribution is to enjoy one's food! The quality of diet in earlier years will have helped to determine our physical condition at this stage. As has been said earlier, energy-producing foods such as carbohydrates are not needed in such quantity as earlier in life. The value of what are called primary foods — fruit, meat, fish, vegetables, whole cereals — should be recognized in the selection of diet. Elderly people should drink more rather than less than before. If the diet is reasonably well-balanced, fewer pills will be required. Eating small meals more frequently has been found helpful by some.

The place of *bed rest* for the aged has come in for a change of viewpoint in recent years. In modern surgery, the tendency has been in many cases to get the patient moving gently as soon as possible. Of course certain physical conditions demand bed rest, and the medical practitioner may prescribe this. But when a person is reasonably fit, undue rest in bed may prove to be a liability rather than an asset.

It is physically harmful to lie for hours in bed, hardly moving a muscle. We must not constantly rest simply because we are old. Those who remain active are the ones who retain the best health. Not only does excessive bed rest adversely affect our morale and make us feel less physically fit than we are, but it can lead to other complications. Incontinence occurs more among those largely confined to bed, than among the more active.

HOW MUCH SLEEP?

The amount of sleep required by an aging person varies widely with the individual. Usually as we grow older, we do not sleep as deeply or as well as before. Some are chronically poor sleepers, and in advancing years they find sleep even more fugitive. Others, who are good sleepers, retain that enviable gift right to the end. Still others do not require a great deal of sleep. I knew a man who went to the mission field late in life who said that if he got more than four hours' sleep a night, he could jump over the moon.

It is generally conceded that older people wake up more frequently, and find that they sleep less than in former years. Some compensate for the sleepless night hours by retiring earlier or rising later. A midday siesta can be a helpful supplement.

"The sleep of the working man is pleasant, whether he eats little or much. But the full stomach of the rich man does not allow him to sleep" (Ecclesiastes 5:12). This is probably a piece of autobiography by the Preacher, but it can have a message for us who are aging. Attention to our eating habits, especially late in the day, might prove helpful for our sleeping hours.

Nothing destroys sleep more effectively than worry, especially if it focuses on our difficulty in sleeping. That kind of anxiety can prove self-fulfilling. It has been claimed that even if we do not sleep well, we get the benefit of 85 percent of the refreshment of normal sleeping hours, provided we are relaxed and do not worry about our wakefulness.

Actually, although we ourselves may take some convincing, most of us get more sleep than we realize. Checking oneself on this point with a chiming clock is illuminating! Of itself, a degree of sleep-lessness is not very harmful — especially in old age — if one lies resting quietly and thinking about more edifying things than insomnia! Another aid to sleep is to rise and make a hot drink and visit the toilet. Some find light reading helpful.

Sleeping pills should be used as a last resort, not as a habit, although mild doses may at times be needed.

Undoubtedly one of the best preparations for a good night's rest is, when physically possible, to have a reasonably active day. It must be borne in mind that sleep after inactivity is not the equivalent of rest after exertion, in which resources are replenished, and a reserve of potential energy stored up for the next day.

In his *Quest for Serenity,* G.H. Morling makes this suggestion: "What if sleep eludes you? Remember the insomnia of God. Behold, He neither slumbers nor sleeps" (Psalm 121:4).

Amy Wilson Carmichael of India, who knew more than her share of illness and insomnia, shared her experience:

> There may be no good reason for sleeplessness; the clamours of acute pain have passed. How futile, then, is this way of spending time, a way that will make tomorrow so much harder . . .
> And still we do not sleep. Why?
> I have found that in the end, prayer is answered, if not by sleep, then in something even better, the peace that passes all understanding; peace without explanation, peace that can take the edge off the morning's weariness and make the impossible possible. It is the old word turned into blessed fact, ''When He giveth quietness, who then can make trouble?''[1]

KEEPING FIT

Hard and vigorous exercise may not be desirable or necessary for those in the upper age bracket, but some form of regular exercise suited to their condition is essential if maximum health is to be maintained. Inactivity is no necessary accompaniment of old age.

In an article in *The Toronto Star* (18 September 1980), Dr. Herbert de Vries of the Gerontology Center of the University of Southern California had this to say, "The elderly can gain up to 30 percent of their youthful vigor just by exercising regularly." This opinion was the result of ten years of research and investigation into the ways exercise affects aging.

He recommended walking as the best exercise for regaining vitality. It is the easiest way for an older person to obtain exercise, as it is so flexible. One can walk fast or slow; alone or in company; gently or vigorously; in the park or on the street; in summer and in winter. It calls for no skill and involves no equipment—except a walking stick. You can stop for a rest at will.

Running or jogging would be a risky form of exercise for the aging, unless it has been engaged in regularly, and has been sanctioned by a physician.

One rule for all exercise is that it should be carried out with moderation. It should not be pursued beyond the point when one is comfortably tired.

Exercise has the effect of increasing the metabolic rate. That enables the body to change more food into available energy. The more the body is exercised and used, the better condition it will be in.

The following interesting report appeared in *The South African Digest* (17 October 1980). "Twelve of the highest and toughest mountains in the Swiss Alps—including the 'Killer' mountain, Eiger—have recently been conquered by a seventy year old South African, climbing vertical ice in near impossible conditions." He certainly exploded the myth that capacity for either physical or mental activity must diminish when one attains a certain age.

We need not fear engaging in either physical or mental activity (illness or disease excepted), provided prudence is exercised. If we gradually increase our activity, we will discover an increase in our power to achieve as well.

There is a very real difference between rest after such physical effort and after inactivity. All rest does not restore depleted physical energy. Who has not observed that on rising in the morning the body is sluggish and inelastic, and the joints stiff? Only after we engage in some form of activity do we begin to limber up. If we remain in bed too long, far from increasing and renewing our physical capacity, it will tend to have the opposite effect. On the other hand, rest after effort both restores and renews.

One medical group studied the progress of a number of people who began a regimen of extensive exercises at the age of sixty. They were an ordinary cross-section of the public and not athletes. The team kept track of their progress until they were seventy. Their report revealed that all showed improved performance. They were actually better physiologically at seventy than they had been at sixty. Here is solid encouragement for us to adopt some form of regular exercise, however mild the form it takes.[2]

NOTES

1. Amy W. Carmichael, *Rose from Briar* (London: SPCK, 1933), pp. 192-93. Taken from copyrighted material used by permission of the Christian Literature Crusade, Fort Washington, Pa., 19034.
2. Irene Gore, *Age and Vitality* (London: Unwin, 1973), p. 80.

13

Disturbers of the Peace

Even earnest Christians who have lived consistently godly lives sometimes encounter distressing experiences when, through the normal processes of senescence, their mental powers begin to wane and are, therefore, less under volitional control. For example, some good people are worried by *the intrusion of unwelcome thoughts*. Sometimes, all unbidden, even obscene or blasphemous thoughts that are entirely out of character invade the mind.

Or the problem may be the eruption of unwarranted fears. One esteemed friend told me that occasionally fears concerning the safety of his adult children and their families disturb him. Though he knows those fears are baseless, it is nonetheless disturbing at the time.

It should be borne in mind that such conditions are not culpable in any sense, and are no cause for self-reproach. Their origin is hell, not heaven, and they should be treated accordingly.

We are responsible only for those areas of our lives that are under our control. When such thoughts come unbidden, we should immediately reject them, and turn them over to the Lord. This is Peter's sage counsel: "Casting all your anxiety upon Him, because He cares for you" (1 Peter 5:7).

All of your care—tomorrow with its problems,
The lengthening shadows of the passing days,
The secret fears, of failure, weakness, suffering,
Of grief and loss, and straitened lonely ways.
Leave it with Him, your future He will share,
For you are His, the object of His care.

Joan Suisted

With more time for reflection, one sees more past events with a strange clarity. In the rush and bustle of earlier life it was compara-

93

tively easy to shrug things off, but now, in retrospect, they can return and fill us with vain regrets.

Of course, in some cases there is genuine reason for regret. Where that is the case, it should be confessed to God, and where necessary, confession and restitution made to those who have suffered by our action. Having done all we can to right the situation, we should accept the promised cleansing of the blood of Christ (1 John 1:9), and then purposefully banish the subject from our minds. Steadfastly refuse the temptation to reopen the subject. Why should we remember what God has forgotten?

PUTTING THINGS RIGHT

Where those whom we may have hurt or offended are dead, there is only one thing to do. Since no restitution to them is possible, we should express our genuine sorrow to God, accept His forgiveness, and consider the matter closed. It is futile to mar our present fellowship with God by entertaining the ghosts of vain regrets.

On one occasion when I was speaking at a conference in California, an elderly man, hearing that I hailed from New Zealand, told me that he had lived there fifty years previously, in a city in which I also had lived. In the course of conversation he asked whether I had known a lawyer named John Wilkinson. "Know him?" I replied, "I used to work with him." And so we talked of mutual acquaintances.

At the end of the conference he enquired if Mr. Wilkinson's son was still living. I told him that he had died. "Oh, I am sorry!" he said. When I asked why he was sorry, he hesitated — and then said, "When I left Dunedin, I owed Mr. Wilkinson a sum of money which I have never repaid. God has been speaking to me about it during this conference, and I thought I would pay whatever was right to the son. Now it is too late. What can I do?"

I suggested that he donate the appropriate amount to some Christian work. God would accept that as an evidence of his repentance and would, for Christ's sake, forgive his sin. He later told me he had done that, and his joy in God was restored.

What a commentary on our heavenly Father's personal care that He should bring together probably the only two people out of America's 230 million who had known John Wilkinson fifty years before, in order that an old man might have the opportunity of putting right a fifty-year-old sin.

Unresolved feelings about omissions or actual wrongdoing in the past, whether real or imagined, can create deep psychological disturbances. Painful memories can invade and disturb our sleeping hours. But there is psychological release when those disturbing thoughts and the accompanying remorse are squarely faced and dealt with on scriptural lines.

It is very possible that the real trouble is *false guilt* that comes from Satan and not from God. Satan is a dirty fighter, and he delights to attack a believer when he is least able to defend himself against "the flaming missiles of the evil one" (Ephesians 6:16).

Few things are more acutely distressing than being tormented by the accusing voice of a weak or guilty conscience. If that is our case, and conscience condemns, we should remember that upon repentance and confession, *the worst sin can be forgiven.* Its guilt then passes immediately and forever from the conscience.

This is the glorious message of Hebrews 9:13-14 (italics added):

"If the blood of goats and bulls and the ashes of a heifer sprinkling those who have been defiled, sanctify for the cleansing of the flesh, *how much more* will the blood of Christ, who through the eternal Spirit offered Himself without blemish to God, *cleanse your conscience* from dead works to serve the living God?"

The Holy Spirit here emphasizes the potency of the blood of Christ to effect a complete cleansing. Note the "how much more," which gives added force to the superiority of the offering of Christ's sinless and sentient life, over the offering of the lives of dumb animals. All the benefits of Christ's atoning death are available to the feeblest believer who comes to Him with the weakest faith.

ANXIETY, FAITHLESS AND FUTILE

One of the very real problems that faces those whose income is reduced through redundancy, unemployment, or retirement is the tendency to be anxious and worry about the future. It is a very natural thing for the elderly to worry about the many variables of their old age. For such a universal problem, it is not surprising that our Lord had sage counsel to give.

For this reason I say to you, do not be anxious for your life, as to what you shall eat, or what you shall drink; nor for your body, as to what you shall put on. Is not life more than food, and the body than clothing?

> Look at the birds of the air, that they do not sow, neither do they reap, nor gather into barns, and yet your heavenly Father feeds them. Are you not worth much more than they?
>
> And which of you by being anxious can add a single cubit to his life's span? And why are you anxious about clothing? . . .
>
> *Do not be anxious* then, saying, "What shall we eat?" or "What shall we drink?" or "With what will we clothe ourselves?" . . . Your heavenly Father knows that you need all these things. . . .
>
> Therefore *do not be anxious* for tomorrow; for tomorrow will care for itself. Each day has enough trouble of its own [Matthew 6:25-34, italics added].

In this vivid passage, Jesus is not denouncing prudent forethought. That is wise and praiseworthy. It is not concern, but *overconcern* that He forbids. The tenses of the verbs He used are significant. In verse 25 the meaning is, "stop worrying!" If the habit already has you in its grip, stop it! In verse 31, however, the meaning is, "Don't worry," or "Never worry." If worry is not yet habitual, don't let it grip you. No matter what happens, don't worry. Since Christ commands it, then through the enabling of the Holy Spirit, it is a possible goal.

The Lord appeals to his Father's providential and parental care as a ground for abandoning anxiety about temporal or other concerns. The Father's care for the lower creation is an argument for His provision for the higher creation. With such a Father, *worry is needless*. Moreover, *worry is futile* because it can neither recall and undo the past, nor can it avert disaster or evade the difficulties that loom in the future. Worry about *present* concerns is counterproductive, and is more likely to produce ulcers and thrombosis than solutions. It only serves to impair our judgment and thus render us less competent to make sound decisions.

Most serious of all, *worry is faithless*. To Jesus, worry and anxiety were not amiable hereditary weaknesses that we must learn to live with, but a sinful lack of faith and confidence in His Father. This is no small matter, since "without faith it is impossible to please Him" (Hebrews 11:6).

In my office I used to have a motto that seldom failed to draw comment. It ran: WHY TRUST WHEN YOU CAN WORRY? Almost invariably visitors would assert that the words were the wrong way round—and so they were. But their reversal served to draw attention to the fact that many of us are more prone to worry faithlessly about our problems than to trust God to solve them. We trust God for the stupendously important matter of our salvation, and then are strangely timid about trusting Him for our other, much less important concerns.

Trust and worry cannot sleep in the same bed. They are irreconcilably antagonistic. The one negates the other. And we should remember that *anxiety is unfilial* as well as unbelieving.[1]

The crux of our Lord's teaching on this subject is in Matthew 6:33—"Seek first His Kingdom and His righteousness; and all these things shall be added to you."

The lesson is that if we give priority to God and the interests of His Kingdom, if we have as our goal the attainment of holy character, we need have no anxiety. The Father will supply everything really necessary.

Trust in the heavenly Father's care will bring serenity and tranquility. That does not mean that our faith will not be tested, but it will be able to surmount the severest test.

"Why add tomorrow's possible anxieties to the very real ones of today?" He urges. Why increase today's load by antedating tomorrow's troubles? "Therefore, do not be anxious for tomorrow; for tomorrow will care for itself" (Matthew 6:34).

From "The Effects of Prayer"

Why, wherefore should we do ourselves this wrong,
Or others, that we are not always strong;
That we are ever overborne with care;
That we should ever weak or heartless be,
Anxious or troubled, when with us is prayer,
And joy, and strength, and courage are with thee!

Richard Chenevix Trench

BOREDOM

Especially for those who have led a busy life and suddenly find themselves in retirement, simple boredom can be a very real malady. The days present no new challenge. The hours drag, because although there may be activity, it is not meaningful, and a sense of purposelessness pervades the days.

This condition of mind tends to affect most severely those who have not cultivated in earlier years mental interests or pursuits that can be carried over into old age — those who lack the inner power to generate new pursuits and interests. That unwelcome possibility should stimulate any readers who have not yet reached old age to set to work immediately and prepare ahead for what must inevitably ensue.

One of the most effective ways of overcoming boredom is to interest oneself in the concerns of others, especially of the lonely, disabled, or underprivileged. The alternative, self-occupation, always induces a self-pity that should be treated with as little consideration as a noxious weed, for that is really what it is. If we frequently and vocally indulge in self-pity, we will discover that to be the surest way of forfeiting sympathy from others.

One danger is that when we ourselves are bored, we may become boring — a condition that will inevitably diminish social intercourse. Old people are not the only ones who tend to be boring, but the gradual narrowing of outside contacts and the shrinking of areas of involvement naturally tend to limit the topics of conversation. That is a potent argument for continuing to broaden one's reading. The person whose mental pabulum is confined to the newspaper is the one who is likely to express the same views and repeat the same stories. That can become boring.

Aging people need not become less stimulating, intelligent, and interesting simply because they are old. If they will only take the pains to continue to develop their capacities, they will find that they retain the potential for creating new interests and following new as well as old pursuits. That will provide them with new topics of conversation and will make them a valued social asset rather than a liability.

LONELINESS

An increasing sense of loneliness is not infrequently a painful accompaniment of the weight of years. As physical limitations cause contacts with the outer world to contract, and our contemporaries pass on one by one, some degree of loneliness is inevitable, and is one of the minuses of old age. Although loneliness is not the sole prerogative of the elderly, it is especially likely to overtake the long-lived.

Those who will be the most fortunate in this respect will be those who in earlier years have cultivated close friendships with a number of people. It is a simple fact of life that as one grows older, the circle becomes narrower and visitors become fewer for one reason or another; our friends become less mobile or move away. Human friendships are subject to the ravages of time.

A social investigator in Europe discovered that 30 percent of retired people when questioned said that they were never visited by anyone! The rapid increase in high-rise apartment living is making the problem of loneliness much more acute.

It is when we lose loved ones, especially a partner of a happy marriage, that loneliness reaches its nadir. The closer the bond, the deeper the grief will be, and the more devastating the subsequent loneliness. Being a Christian does not dehumanize one. The sense of loss is as real and deep to the Christian as to anyone else, but for him there are compensating factors unknown by the non-Christian.

The person who in the course of his working life has been accustomed to the companionable talk of friends and workmates, and then suddenly has that social intercourse cut off through retirement, is likely to feel acutely lonely — in the early stages at least. It may be that they were lonely before without fully realizing it, because life was so full and absorbing. But increased leisure may serve to bring this fact into painful relief. It has been observed that social integration becomes more difficult, though by no means impossible, after the age of fifty.

One can be very lonely even in a merry crowd. Byron expressed his own poignant experience in his poem:

> Although gay companions o'er the bowl
> Dispel awhile the sense of ill,
> Though pleasures fill the maddening soul,
> The heart, the heart is lonely still.
>
> There is a mystery in human hearts,
> And though we be encircled by a host
> Of those who love us well and are beloved,
> To every one of us from time to time,
> There comes a sense of utter loneliness.

THE COMPENSATING PRESENCE

Whether we are old or young, the sense of deep inner loneliness that seems to have invaded the youth of this generation to a surprising degree, will find its fullest relief only in living fellowship with the ever-present Christ. We are given abundant assurance of that joyous possibility in the Scriptures, but it remains for us to believe those promises and make them our own by a restful faith. Here are a selection of exceedingly great and precious promises that await our appropriation:

- "My presence shall go with you, and I will give you rest" (Exodus 33:14).
- "Even though I walk through the valley of the shadow of death, I fear no evil; for Thou art with me" (Psalm 23:4).
- "Do not fear, for I am with you; Do not anxiously look about you, for I am your God. I will strengthen you, surely I will help you, Surely I will uphold you with My righteous hand" (Isaiah 41:10).
- "Behold, the virgin shall be with child, and shall bear a Son, and they shall call His name Immanuel, which translated means, 'God with us' " (Matthew 1:23).
- "Lo, I am with you always, even to the end of the age" (Matthew 28:20).
- "He Himself has said, 'I will never desert you, nor will I ever forsake you,' so that we confidently say, 'The Lord is my Helper, I will not be afraid. What shall man do to me?' " (Hebrews 13:5-6).

Prayer cancels loneliness, for not only does it deepen fellowship with God, but it enables us to rove the world in our sympathies and intercessions. However, self-centered prayers for ourselves and our own petty interests will not achieve that. It is when our hearts are enlarged, and we embrace in our prayers a widening circle of needy people, that we discover prayer does really cancel loneliness. To feed on our own loneliness is self-defeating.

The happiest — and often the healthiest — aging people, are those who are not self-occupied, for that is a self-fulfilling recipe for loneliness. Our happiness and enjoyment of growing old depends far more on our *attitudes* that on our *circumstances,* however adverse they may be. Many helpless invalids are a pleasure to visit because they are outgoing, not self-occupied.

With others the case is different. The visitor is treated to a catalogue of aches and pains and real — or imagined — grievances of the past as well as the present. Those may indeed be very real to them, but the recital in no way relieves them, but only serves to make the visitor less enthusiastic about a return visit.

Loneliness is an especially acute reality to unmarried or widowed people. They have no partner with whom they can share joys and sorrows or discuss problems of mutual concern. Since there are three times as many widows as widowers, this is a predominantly feminine problem. It is of passing interest that the Bible has much to say about widows and provision for them, but little about widowers.

The single or widowed should have a special place in the hearts of their fellow-Christians. They have to travel the same road as others, but often lack the supportive love a married partner can give. That makes it all the more necessary for them to cherish or establish warm family and social relationships. A friend who can be a close and reliable confidant can provide such support, and that should be made a matter of prayer.

We should not readily resign ourselves to loneliness — there are active steps that can be taken to alleviate it. The common tendency to withdraw into oneself must be strenuously resisted if we are to escape the arid desert of loneliness.

Losing oneself in the interests and concerns of others, setting desires and ambitions on objectives outside oneself, is the road to relief from our isolation.

At a party the conversation turned to the subject of old age. One friend asked another, "What is it like to be old?" The other was flustered because the question had been addressed to *her*, and ignored it. Ten minutes later she called the friend over and whispered under the party hubbub, "Above all, it's the loneliness!" Many others would have returned the same answer. But there is a panacea.

Writing in *Who Walk Alone*, Margaret Evening strikes an optimistic note that does not blink at the facts.

> The time comes to most of us when, whether we like it or not, old age and failing powers force us into solitude. Many people dread this time, and of course we cannot lapse into idleness and become an increasing burden to others. We must keep going while we can. But inevitably we shall become more and more alone.

> If we have longed for solitude and learned to love it because we find God there, it should be that the last years of a long life will be the happiest of all, lived so close to Him that His love and life can shine through us to countless souls.[3]

Another writer suggests that loneliness may sometimes be one of God's methods of securing our undivided attention. It will indeed prove a blessing if it makes us more responsive to His presence and obedient to His will.

> Man either transcends his own loneliness in a new encounter with God, or he succumbs to its agony which, in extreme cases, can end in final despair.[4]
>
> Alfons Deeken

Let us seek, then, that fresh encounter with God.

SELF-OCCUPATION

Nothing is easier for the aging person who is growing increasingly infirm and experiencing some depression as a result, than to turn inward and become self-occupied. That attitude of mind only exacerbates the problem. It is when with firm purpose we turn away from our own griefs, aches, and ailments, and busy ourselves to relieve those of others, that we will obtain relief from our own. It was when Job prayed for his friends that the Lord restored his fortunes (Job 42:10). "Taking the griefs of others inoculates me against my own," was the prescription of one sufferer who had triumphed over adverse circumstances.

When Josephine Butler, one of the greatest social workers of her day, lost her only child, an old Quaker to whom she turned for help in her grief reminded her that there were many other young hearts who needed mother-love. He directed her to a certain house where forty young people who had been rescued from moral evil were being cared for.

Josephine rose above her own grief and gave herself with abandon to care for these young lives. Someone said of her, "She did not bear her grief, she set it to music." Her life was an exemplification of the Marechale's hymn:

Turn your trouble into treasure,
Turn your sorrow into song,
Then the world will know the measure
In which you to Christ belong.

Catherine Booth Clibborn

In 1953 I was traveling in Asia with Fred Mitchell, then British director of the China Inland Mission and chairman of the English Keswick Convention. When we had completed our mission tour, we separated at Singapore. Fred flew to London in one of the new "Comet" aircraft, while I went to Hong Kong. When the Comet got as far as Calcutta, it exploded and all aboard were killed.

Mrs. Mitchell was frail in body, and for a time the shock prostrated her. As she faced the lonely future and sought God's will for her life, He brought to her mind the fact that she was only one of thousands of widows who were in a similar position. Then came the suggestion, "Why not share your testimony to My goodness and care, with some of these other widows?"

So began a quiet, but very fruitful ministry to grieving widows, many of whom knew nothing of the comfort of the God, who said, "As one whom his mother comforts, so I will comfort you" (Isaiah 66:13). When she read in the newspaper of women who had been widowed — often under tragic circumstances — she wrote to them, sharing her faith sympathetically. She turned her sorrow into song.

Ask God to give the skill
For comfort's art,
That thou may'st consecrated be
And set apart
Unto a life of sympathy;
For heavy is the weight of ill
For every heart,
And comforters are needed much,
Of Christ-like touch

Peter McRostie

But not all are prepared to stir themselves out of their own self-occupation to help others. Stanley Jones tells how he once asked elderly people in a sanitorium to take garments and sew for China relief. He expected there would be a great eagerness to respond, as busy people outside had responded magnificently. Now these old people had all the time there was on their hands, but to his amazement not one responded.[5]

That was one of the reasons why they were in the home — they were so busy thinking about their own ailments and troubles that they had no time for others. Let us ask God to give us

> A heart at leisure from itself,
> To soothe and sympathize

LOSS OF INDEPENDENCE

The ideal state for aging people in reasonable health is for them to retain their independence for as long as is comfortably possible. To most, though not all, their independence is increasingly prized as the need for dependence on others looms on the horizon.

But the time usually comes when increasing frailty or ill health makes that impossible. Then comes the perplexing decision concerning the future, and for some, decision-making becomes increasingly difficult. Retirement homes are one alternative, or some caring relative or friend may offer a home. The latter may appear very attractive when the alternative is considered, but it should be thought through very carefully. Experience teaches that with the best will in the world on both sides, tensions can arise.

If it is possible to live near, but not actually in the home of the relative, that may prove a satisfactory solution. The wisest parent living with a relative can very easily be tempted to interfere in the conduct of the home when difficulties arise, but that is usually counterproductive. Even if actual interference is avoided, unspoken criticism can become strangely vocal, and create a tense atmosphere. It is no easy lesson for an aged person to realize that their children are mature adults and thoroughly responsible.

If one accepts the invitation to live with relatives the change of role will call for a great deal of adaptation and understanding on both sides. To become a guest in another's home, even if it is one's own child — instead of being master or mistress — can be a traumatic experience. Leaving familiar scenes, parting with familiar furniture and other treasures, relinquishing cherished responsibilities, being welcomed, but not really needed in a physical sense — even in the family where one is loved—cannot but cause shock and a sense of deprivation.

One possible cause of contention can arise from the fact that the third generation holds very different ideas of discipline and standards from our own. Two spheres in which it will be wise for the grandparent to withhold critical comment would be in the areas of finance and radio or television. Young people of today have never known the financial stringency that many of us had to face in our youth. That is not their fault, for they, as we, are the victims of the current culture.

The youth of today have been brought up in a world inured to loud music; for many, the louder the better. Even some lovers of classical music must have it considerably amplified to really enjoy it. Although we may neither approve nor enjoy, it is the part of wisdom to refrain from adverse comment in the home in which we are guests, not owners. Criticism seldom improves the atmosphere.

The elderly will more likely be asked for their advice if they do not insist on proffering it. If our attitude to our young people is judgmental rather than understanding and sympathetic, we need not be surprised if they do not open their hearts to us.

As for those who are contemplating opening their homes to an elderly relative, they are considering a worthy and sacrificial act, appreciated by the Lord. But it would be wise first to count the cost very carefully, and face realistically the long-term possibilities. In many cases where such an invitation has been offered spontaneously and generously, but without careful forethought, it has been regretted later.

It should be stressed that adding a mature aged person to a household can be an unmitigated blessing; but on the other hand, considerable strain and tension can be generated. If, however, the circumstances are reasonable, the mutual attitudes good, and there is a clear understanding of the respective roles, the prognosis is good.

The role of grandparents in the Eastern culture is more honorable and respected than in our own. However, if wisdom and restraint are exercised, there is no reason why that should not be the case in the West as well. It is when grandparents step out of their role in the home in which they are now the guests of their mature adult children, that trouble begins.

THE NEED TO BE NEEDED

One of the paramount needs of the elderly as physical powers wane and social contacts diminish, is the need to be needed; of being assured that they are still able to make some small contribution to the common good. Grandparents can often find that need supplied in service rendered to their families. Those who can impart that confidence to the aging are doing more than they realize to bring cheer and a sense of well-being.

A study group from the University of Iowa devoted their research toward ascertaining the basic needs of those who were living in retirement.[6] Their findings were generally predictable, but some are worthy of note.

Aging people whose status in life has diminished either through retirement or age need to be reassured that they are regarded as worthy individuals in their own right. If they can be made to feel that they are an asset to the community and not a liability, that will go a long way to restore confidence and stimulate fresh endeavor.

They need to have both the desire and the opportunity for performing some socially useful service, however small. "Meals on wheels" is a case in point. Normal companionship, especially with those of the same generation is a *sine qua non,* indispensable. Opportunity for self-expression with an accompanying sense of achievement is another need.

As frailty increases, there is a growing necessity for protection, suitable living conditions, and loving care, whether in a family situation or in a retirement home.

Mental stimulation is another essential if the elderly person is not to drift into a vegetable-like existence. In some ways television has proved a great boon to the old, especially if it provides mental stimulation; but many programs, however, have the opposite tendency. TV can be an opiate, allowing little opportunity for self-expression. It is inert, and encourages inactivity rather than movement. Further, it creates emotions for which there is no adequate outlet. Again, it is a lone experience and provides no companionship. Anyone who interrupts a favorite serial is not at all popular. For TV to exercise the beneficent influence of which it is capable, a firm hand should be kept on the control knob!

NOTES

1. J. Oswald Sanders, *The World's Greatest Sermon* (London: Marshall, Morgan & Scott, 1972), p. 126.
2. Morton Puner, *To the Good, Long Life* (London: Macmillan, 1974), p. 110.
3. Margaret Evening, *Who Walk Alone* (London: Hodder & Stoughton, 1974), p. 182.
4. Alfons Deeken, *Growing Old* (New York: Paulist, 1972), p. 28.
5. Stanley E. Jones, *Growing Spiritually* (Nashville: Abingdon, 1953), p. 187.
6. Puner, p. 174.

14

The Poignancy of Bereavement

Sooner or later the pain of bereavement will be our lot. Married people must face the certainty that one or the other will go through this experience. With the life expectancy of women being about five years longer than that of men, it is the wife who will more likely be the survivor.

It is not morbid to consider this eventuality, for although we cannot prepare fully for it, it is wisdom to learn what we may expect. Where there has been a long period of painful illness, there may even be a sense of relief when death ensues. But when it has not been anticipated and it comes suddenly, it often leaves the survivor stunned and numb.

None of us is really prepared for this unexpected and unwelcome visitation. Our ability to cope with death triumphantly depends in large measure on the support of our family and friends, and on the vitality of our Christian faith and experience.

Facing the fact that grief and bereavement are bound to come to us eventually will save us from falling into self-pity or thinking that we are the objects of special judgment. Grief comes to others, and we have no grounds for believing that we will be the exception.

The experience can either sweeten or sour us, and we ourselves determine which it shall be. Reason is not a great help in meeting grief, for it is an emotional rather than a logical experience. But the will has an important part to play.

"Sorrow does color life, doesn't it," said one friend to another who had been bereaved. "Yes it does," was the answer, "and I intend to choose the colors." Such a reply was a good prognosis for the days ahead.

Isaiah the prophet gives comforting insight into the problem of grief and bereavement in the familiar words: "Surely our griefs He

Himself bore, and our sorrows He carried'' (Isaiah 53:4). This reminds us that our sympathetic Lord is very close to us in our hour of need. ''We do not have a high priest who cannot sympathize with our weaknesses, but one who has been tempted in all things as we are, yet without sin'' (Hebrews 4:15). It is blessedly true that ''in all the pangs that rend the heart, the Man of Sorrows shares a part.''

It is into His compassionate hands that we can surrender our grief. His ability to enter into the sorrows of His friends was displayed when He met Mary and the friends who were mourning with her. ''When Jesus therefore saw her weeping . . . He was deeply moved in spirit, and was troubled, and said, 'Where have you laid him?' They said to Him, 'Lord, come and see.' Jesus wept. And so the Jews were saying, 'Behold, how He loved him!' '' (John 11:33-36). His were not the synthetic tears of the TV screen. The word ''wept'' conveyed the idea of tears streaming down His face. What a picture — a weeping God!

How safe it is to come to Him in our sorrow and commit our grief to One who so fully understands and cares. Having committed it to Him, leave it there finally and permanently. The deep hurt remains, but the compensating presence and ministry of ''the God of all comfort'' (2 Corinthians 1:3) will support us in our grief, and transform it into triumph — even though the triumph may be tear-bedewed.

A bereaved friend, whose deeply-loved son of fifteen was killed in a motor accident, bore this testimony: ''In the furnace of our affliction, as the flames leaped high and hot, there walked One like the Son of God, and we were not consumed. This is grace — God's grace. Full, glorious, true — promised in His Word, provided in His love, and constantly available to any trusting child in need.''[1]

When he was a young married man, Prebendary Webb-Peploe, a noted British preacher, took his little family to the seaside for a holiday. One of his little children was drowned. He returned to the city devastated with grief. In his distress he knelt at the desk in his study and poured out his grief before God. He pleaded with God to make His grace sufficient for him in his deep need. But no comfort came. The sense of desolation was still as acute as ever.

Through his tears, he looked up at the familiar text on the wall above the mantelpiece, but now with a new interest. The text was:

"My grace IS sufficient for thee" (2 Corinthians 12:9). For the first time he noticed that the IS was printed in large letters. Light dawned. "Lord, here have I been asking you to *make* your grace sufficient for me in my loss, and all the time you have been telling me that it *IS* sufficient. I now appropriate for myself your sufficient grace." His act of faith was immediately rewarded. Although the sense of loss was no less, the compensating comfort of God flooded his heart and he had peace.

When we thus embrace the will of God, paradoxically it proves sweet and acceptable. If, like the psalmist, we "refuse to be comforted," (Psalm 77:2), we are left without resource to meet the hours of desolation.

EXPRESS YOUR GRIEF

It is right to express our grief unashamedly. Jesus wept. To deny, suppress, or try to ignore grief will only delay the painful journey back to everyday life. We do not have to adopt an artificial or stoical attitude. Expressing feelings in a natural way can be a catharsis. Bereavement is indeed a lonely sorrow, and though we may be surrounded by loved and sympathetic friends, we are still alone in our grief. But as our Lord said, we are alone — yet not alone, for He is with us (John 16:32).

EACH DAY A CHALLENGE

In the September 1980 issue of *Readers Digest,* Daphne du Maurier wrote, "Time heals all wounds," but added that that is true only if there is no suppuration within. To be bitter makes the wounds fester. We can hug our sorrows and refuse to surrender them — but that will only make us more miserable, affect the lives of those near to us, and mar our Christian testimony.

In the early days of our loss, it is difficult not to blame ourselves, or others, but that attitude only spreads the infection.

"I would say to those who mourn," Miss du Maurier continued, "look on each day that comes as a challenge, as a test of courage. The pain will come in waves, some days worse than others, for no apparent reason. Accept the pain. Little by little you will find new strength, new vision, born of the very pain and loneliness which seem, at first, impossible to master."

The best therapy for our grief and loneliness is to form close and warm relationships, especially with those who are sharing the same experience. The temptation to withdraw into our sad selves is to be strongly resisted.

Far from being a tribute to the memory of a departed loved one, for someone to go around moping and indulging in an orgy of self-pity is in reality disloyalty to their memory. That is the last thing they would wish. Excessive grief can actually be a subtle form of self-pity. Most who have lost deeply loved ones find that keeping busily occupied, and taking an interest in the concerns of others, gradually dulls the keen edge of our grief.

> From distant years, if tearful memories rise,
> Dear scenes, and faces known on earth no more,
> Unchanging Friend, to Thee I turn my eyes,
> And all my sadness on Thy bosom pour.

Bishop Frank Houghton, former general director of the China Inland Mission, in writing to Miss Amy Carmichael of the Dohnavur Fellowship of India concerning the death of his youngest sister, demonstrated a wholesome attitude to bereavement.

> Many of our friends in their letters of sympathy speak of God's mysterious ways, and I know there is an element of mystery. But I shrink from the suggestion that our father has done anything which needs to be explained. What He has done is the best, because He has done it, and I pray that as a family we may not cast about for explanations of the mystery, but exult in the Holy Spirit, and say, 'I thank Thee Father . . . Even so Father . . .'
>
> It suggests a lack of confidence in Him if we find it necessary to try to understand all He does.
>
> Will it not bring greater joy to tell Him that we need no explanation because we know Him?

"As for God, his way is perfect" (Psalm 18:30, KJV). If His way is perfect, we need no explanation.

THE WIDOW'S PLIGHT

"Widowhood is a kind of retirement," said Paul Tournier, "the retirement of a woman from her job as a wife." All too often, meaning goes out of life with the death of the partner, whether husband or wife, and the relict faces a lonely desert-like prospect. "Widowhood [the term can include the widower] is always a terrible trial," Tournier continues, "and in addition to the emotional shock and separation, there is always considerable disturbance in the social and personal life of the surviving partner." Viewed from any angle, the lot of the widow or widower is a solitary sorrow.

It has been the experience of many widows that in the early days of her bereavement she receives a great deal of sympathy and help. At first she is still invited out by friends, but gradually invitations grow fewer, and the number of visiting friends declines.

That is especially true when the husband was popular and used to be the life of the party. Many widows feel, probably without complete justification, that there is some sort of stigma attached to widowhood that adds to the inevitable loneliness.

During the Depression of the thirties, my sister was widowed and left with three small children and no income other than a meager widow's pension. She proved, however, the validity of the reassuring promise of Isaiah 54:4-5: "Fear not, for you will not be put to shame . . . and the reproach of your widowhood you will remember no more. *For your husband is your Maker,* whose name is the LORD of hosts; And your Redeemer is the Holy One of Israel" (italics added).

Although she frequently did not know how the next meal would be provided, she threw her home open to others who were lonely or in distress. In ministering to the needs of others, her own loneliness was somewhat assuaged. Her Maker proved to be both Husband and Provider.

It was Soren Kirkegaard's contention that suffering is incommunicable. There is a very real sense in which the sorrow and suffering of widowhood is incommunicable, and must be borne alone.

Throughout the Bible special note is given to the plight of the widow; and under the Old Covenant, special provision was made for her:

- "You shall not afflict any widow or orphan" (Exodus 22:22)
- "You shall not . . . take a widow's garment in pledge" (Deuteronomy 24:17)

- "When you reap your harvest in your field and have forgotten a sheaf in the field, you shall not go back to get it; it shall be for the alien, the orphan, and for the widow" (Deuteronomy 24:19-21)
- "A father of the fatherless and a judge for the widows, is God in His holy habitation" (Psalm 68:5).

The New Covenant, also, is sympathetic to the widows' plight, and they can take comfort from the fact that God is not indifferent to their sorrow.

In the early church, a situation arose where certain widows appeared to be discriminated against. The divine concern was communicated to the apostles, who took the matter in hand.

A complaint arose on the part of the Hellenistic Jews against the native Hebrews, because their widows were being overlooked in the daily serving of food. And the twelve . . . said, "It is not desirable for us to neglect the word of God in order to serve tables. But select from among you, brethren, seven men of good reputation, full of the Spirit and of wisdom, whom we may put in charge of this task" [Acts 6:1-3].

Both Paul and James give counsel to and concerning widows:

If any woman who is a believer has dependent widows, let her assist them, and let not the church be burdened, so that it may assist those who are widows indeed [1 Timothy 5:16].

This is pure and undefiled religion in the sight of our God and Father, to visit orphans and widows in their distress [James 1:27].

It is the responsibility of the church and its individual members to see that those divine injunctions are honored in spirit as well as in letter.

The plight of the widower, it should be noted, has received much less considerate attention than that of the widow in our society. It is assumed, often wrongly, that he is better able to cope with the situation than is his partner. It is sometimes asserted that a widower is at a premium in social circles, but that is by no means always the case. The facts are far otherwise. Especially if he is not domesticated, old age for a widower can be a very bleak experience.

However happy the marriage may have been, there will always be sorrow, shock, and a sense of loss. If the marriage was not very successful, guilt, remorse, and regret may be added to the natural sorrow, and that may prove more difficult to deal with than the sense of loss itself. Again, resting in the Lord is our resource. Even in such a case, the affirmation still stands: "My grace is sufficient for you" (2 Corinthians 12:9). At this juncture, the loving support of friends and relatives is a great help.

Luke records the story of an old widow of many years standing, who triumphed over the sorrows of her long widowhood.

> There was a prophetess, Anna the daughter of Phanuel, of the tribe of Asher. She was advanced in years, having lived with a husband seven years after her marriage, and then as a widow to the age of eighty-four. And she never left the temple, serving night and day with fastings and prayers.
>
> And at that very moment she came up and began giving thanks to God, and continued to speak of Him to all those who were looking for the redemption of Jerusalem (Luke 2:36-38).

Here was a widow who did not become embittered at the hardness of her lot, but devoted herself wholeheartedly to the service of God in His house. Like Joshua, she spent her time in the place where God manifested Himself to His people. The three activities that filled her life and made her biography worthy of being preserved for us in Scripture, are equally open to us in old age, when physical activity is limited. She occupied her time in serving the Lord, praising Him for His mercies, and continually speaking of Him to others.

NOTES

1. Isabel Fleece, *Not by Accident* (Chicago: Moody, 1964), p. 29.

15

Enemy or Benefactor

In the glow of wholesome youth, and amid the joys and pressures of the thirties and the forties, it was not difficult for most of us to push back in our consciousness such a mysterious and unwelcome thought as that of death. Few accept the approach of death with serenity; most of the time we just try not to think about it.

But with the advent of middle age and more frequent contact with the death of others, it is not so easy to repress the realization of our own mortality. A text such as "It is appointed for men to die once, and after this comes judgment" (Hebrews 9:27) becomes less a theological concept and more an inescapable certainty. To many the thought of death, with its aura of mystery, gives rise to intangible but very real fears, as described in Hebrews 2:15: "those who through fear of death were subject to slavery all their lives."

Christianity neither magnifies nor minimizes death. It is recognized as the inevitable corollary of living. Since it is represented throughout Scripture as the end result of sin, Paul describes it as the last enemy to be destroyed at the second advent of Christ. It is a striking historical fact, however, that the early Christians came to regard death as a benefactor who was going to do them the greatest kindness, rather than as an enemy.

Christianity has not simplified the problem of death, since it has affirmed that death could assail even God, in the person of Christ. It is indeed the last enemy, and yet on the other hand, death is the gateway — the transition to an unending experience of fellowship with the Holy Trinity. The grave is only an underground pathway to heaven.

In Dr. Paul Tournier's view, death for the believer is no longer a curse or punishment. It is the event that is preparatory and necessary to resurrection, a new age of fulfillment.

From the nature of the case, old age and death are inseparable, for death is just the normal consequence of living in a world that has been blighted by sin. Death is never welcome—except where there has been deep suffering or sorrow, when its advent may be hailed with a measure of relief.

Man's unavoidable mortality is a subject about which people are loath to speak. In part, that is because death touches the springs of our deepest emotions, and in part because it always causes shock and finds us unprepared, whether the death is sudden or long-anticipated.

Reaction to either the thought or the reality of death varies widely with the individual and the circumstances. Some are able to face the prospect with serenity because of their vital faith in Christ and their scripturally-based assurance of their own salvation. That is an assurance every Christian can, and should enjoy, but something not all do experience.

Those who face death most confidently and without fear are likely to be people who have fully accepted the fact that death will come to them in due course. Those who have experienced a long and happy life, enriched by a vital Christian faith, are more likely to accept death with a tranquility that will leave a fragrant memory with those who mourn.

Is there not a sense in which the whole of our life is a preparation for death? When we accept the reality of our own death not as something to be discussed objectively, but as something we are going to experience subjectively, our present living will be significantly influenced.

When some lively young people observed their grandmother always reading and meditating on her Bible, one remarked, "Grandma must be cramming for her finals!" The fact is that with the advancing years, the things of earth grow strangely dim, and the things of eternity become gloriously real.

WITH CHRIST—FAR BETTER

Was this not the case with Paul the aged? To him, death was "to depart, and be with Christ, which is far better" (Philippians 1:23, KJV). When the hour of his martyrdom drew near, he faced it with a cheerful serenity: "I am already being poured out as a drink offering, and the time of my departure has come. I have fought the good fight, I have finished the course, I have kept the faith; in the future there is laid up for me the crown of righteousness, which the Lord, the righteous Judge, will award to me on that day" (2 Timothy 4:6-8).

Early historians remarked on the courage and joy with which the Christians faced a cruel death. The note of their triumph was described by Aristides in A.D. 125. Writing to a friend about a new religion called Christianity, he said: "If any righteous man among the Christians passes from this world, they rejoice, and offer thanks to God; and they escort his body with songs of thanksgiving as if he were setting out from one place to another nearby."

Those suffering saints attained a wholesome and triumphant approach to the reality of death, because they had experienced and believed in the power of Christ's resurrection. The stark contrast between their joy and triumph, and the hopeless mourning and wailing of their pagan contemporaries in the presence of death, proved a powerful evangelistic agency.

In an Armistice Day sermon delivered in 1923, Dr. A. C. Dixon, former pastor of the Moody Memorial Church in Chicago, and of Spurgeon's Metropolitan Tabernacle in London, said:

> Man is created an eternal being, and death is God's method of colonization.
>
> There certainly arise conditions in which our heavenly Father knows that it will be best for His children on earth to be removed to another world. This process will continue its work until the Lord of life shall appear and abolish death for all who are His.
>
> The kind of death matters little. Personally I have never prayed, "From sudden death, good Lord deliver us." To me that is the ideal removal. If God should give me a choice between a bullet in battle and death by a lingering disease, I would choose the former without a moment's hesitation.
>
> But I believe when we look back upon the events of life from the heights of glory, we shall see that no mistake was ever made in removing anybody at the wrong time, in the wrong way or to the wrong place.

Henry Francis Lyte, the famous hymn writer who gave us the immortal hymn, *Abide With Me,* expressed his ambition for composing in these words:

> Might verse of mine inspire
> One virtuous aim, one high resolve impart —
> Light in one drooping soul a hallowed fire,
> Or bind one broken heart . . .
> O Thou whose touch can lend
> Life to the dead, The quickening grace supply,
> And grant me, swanlike, my last breath to spend
> In song that may not die.

His aspiration was gloriously realized in *Abide With Me*. On September 4, 1847 he delivered his last sermon. In the evening, he gave to his daughter, with an air of his own composing, the manuscript of his immortal hymn, through which the great desire of his soul was fulfilled. In the original version there is a verse that is seldom sung:

> Thou on my head in early youth didst smile;
> And though rebellious and perverse meanwhile,
> Thou hast not left me, oft as I left Thee,
> On to the close, O Lord, abide with me.

During Lyte's active years, the thought of death brought him much distress. Yet in his dying hours at Nice, faith overmastered fear and he said to the one who cared for him, "Oh, there is nothing terrible in death; Jesus Christ steps down into the grave before me."

After a moment's silent prayer, he pointed upward and added, "O blessed converse! begun on earth, to be perfected soon in paradise! Blessed faith; today piercing through the mists of earth — tomorrow changed to sight! Abiding ever with the Lord." With those words on his lips, Henry Francis Lyte entered the presence of his Lord.

THE LAST ENEMY DESTROYED

Writing to Timothy, Paul refers to Christ as the one "who abolished death, and brought life and immortality to light through the gospel" (2 Timothy 1:10). From one point of view it could be contended that death is anything but abolished. Does it not still invade our homes and break our hearts?

It is interesting that in the verse, "The last enemy that will be abolished is death" (1 Corinthians 15:26), the destruction of death is set forth as a thing yet to occur. But the Greek suggests rather a thing already begun and continuing until it is fully accomplished. The sense is that the last enemy *is being* destroyed. The destruction of death is a thing in the doing. It is not yet completed, but it has begun; it is in progress, and it is certain of being brought to a full end.[2]

The process of death's destruction began with our Lord's resurrection. His death was a death to end death. He died "that through death he might render powerless him who had the power of death, that is the devil" (Hebrews 2:14).

The destruction of death that began with the resurrection will be consummated in our resurrection when the Lord returns. Paul enlarges on that glorious truth in his classic passage on resurrection which climaxes in that marvelous peroration: "Then will come about the saying that is written, 'Death is swallowed up in victory. O death, where is your victory? O death, where is your sting?' The sting of death is sin . . . but thanks be to God, who gives us the victory through our Lord Jesus Christ" (1 Corinthians 15:54-57).

Our Lord has thus "changed the face of death" by bringing life and immortality to light through the gospel. Rather than being master, death is now the servant who opens the door to our eternal home, and closes the door on sin and suffering. "O death, sweet death," said Charles Kingsley, "when wilt thou come and tell me all I want to know?" Death held no terrors for him.

The history of the church is replete with examples of radiant triumph over death. The following testimony from his son, Reuben A. Torrey, Jr., to his father, the world famous evangelist, shows how old age can end victoriously:

> I cannot but feel that the months of declining health were given to my father to enable him to demonstrate the completeness of his victory in Christ Jesus. It is one thing to be a radiant, victorious Christian when one is in his prime, full of vigour and active in service. It is quite another thing to display the same radiant faith and joyous trust in the goodness and wisdom of God when health is failing and one has been set aside from active life.
>
> Throughout the ten months of inactivity caused by poor health, a new experience for my father, he never once manifested the slightest impatience, although it often seemed that there was excuse for impatience and discouragement. His beautiful smile persisted, his op-

timism never faltered, his faith and glad acceptance of God's will became more evident. He gave himself to almost continual Bible study and prayer, and his very presence became a benediction.[3]

> O Grave! Where is thy victory?
> O Death! Where is thy sting?
> O Tomb! Where is thy triumph now?
> Dost evil tidings bring?
> Oh, no! There is no fear in thee —
> For earthly saints rejoice
> In passing through thine open gates

> To hear their Saviour's voice —
> "I am alive for evermore!"
> Death's doors are open wide;
> God's crystal Kingdom gleams with gems
> Upon the other side.

M.S.C.

NOTES

1. Helen C. Dixon, *A. C. Dixon* (New York: Putnam's, 1931) p. 315.
2. J. E. Harris, "The Destruction of Death," *Philadelphia Sunday School Times,* 29 March 1941, p. 351.
3. Reuben A. Torrey, Jr., "Dr. Torrey in His Home," *Moody Monthly,* October 1939, p. 69.

16

The Best Is Yet To Be!

The attitude of the aging Christian should be one of expectancy. We should share the optimism expressed by Browning in his *Rabbi Ben Ezra*.

> Grow old along with me!
> The best is yet to be,
> The last for life, for which the first was made:
> Our times are in His hand
> Who saith, "A whole I planned,
> Youth shows but half; trust God:
> See all, nor be afraid!"

It is a wholly scriptural and Christian conviction that for the obedient disciple, "the best is yet to be." We have by no means exhausted either the resources of God or the possibilities of our own lives. This truth was exemplified in the lives of the ordinary men and women of faith whose records are preserved in God's honor roll.

> All these died in faith, without receiving the promises, but having seen them and having welcomed them from a distance, and having confessed that they were strangers and exiles on the earth. For those who say such things make it clear that they are seeking a country of their own . . . *they desire a better country, that is a heavenly one* [Hebrews 11:13-16, italics added].

There is every reason for us to look forward with joyous expectancy to the consummation of the age in the advent of our Lord or, in the alternative, to our entrance through the portals of our heavenly home by way of death. To be with Christ is far better than anything we have known on this side.

For the believer, the second coming of the Lord will mean the

123

beginnings of the glories of heaven. "I go to prepare a place for you," He said, "And if I go and prepare a place for you, I will come again and receive you to Myself; that where I am, there you may be also" (John 14:2-3).

There is no reason why our closing years should not be cheered and brightened by contemplating the undreamed-of felicity that awaits the Bride of Christ in heaven.

Strangely enough, much of what we know about our heavenly home is negative. Far more is said about the things that are absent from the Father's house than those that are present. In the main, the absences are of those things that, in old age, cause us most pain and distress in this earthly environment.

The word "heaven" means simply, "that which is above," and is used in a threefold sense in Scripture. We read of the atmospheric heavens, the celestial or starry heavens, and the heaven that is the abode of the Holy Trinity. "The LORD's throne is heaven" (Psalm 11:6). Thus for the Christian, heaven is where God is. It is a home that our Lord is especially preparing for His Bride — not servants' quarters, but a bridal suite!

HEAVEN'S ABSENCES

We should note first *the absences from heaven.* In preparing this new home, our Lord removes everything that would spoil our enjoyment or cast gloom on our spirits.

There will be *no more tears,* for "He shall wipe away every tear from their eyes" (Revelation 21:4). He will take heaven's handkerchief and wipe away the tears caused by our sin and failure, as well as those that come through pain, sorrow and bereavement.

Death is forever banished. "There shall no longer be any death" (Revelation 21:4). The "king of terrors" and the "last enemy" will never be able to penetrate the pearly gates. By His death and resurrection, Jesus extracted the sting of death, and now at last it is banished from the universe.

Mourning will be an experience of the past. The ravages of sin and the poignancy of bereavement cause us to mourn here, but there "there shall no longer be any mourning, or crying" (Revelation 21:4).

THE BEST IS YET TO BE!

One of the fears and dreads of our aging years is of the pain that must so often be endured. The worst thing about illness is the pain that accompanies it; but in heaven *"there shall no longer be any . . . pain"* (Revelation 21:4, italics added). In heaven there will be no market for the pain-killing drugs that have proved such a boon to suffering humanity.

No believer will ever again turn on a sickbed. "He showed me a river of the water of life, clear as crystal . . . and on either side of the river was the tree of life . . . and the leaves of the tree were for the healing of the nations" (Revelation 22:1-2).

The world's hunger problem will be solved, for "they shall hunger no more" (Revelation 7:16).

What a blessing night is to the animal and vegetable world. But in heaven, *"there shall no longer be any night"* (Revelation 22:5, italics added). And why will that now essential medium of rest and renewal be abolished? Because in heaven our changed bodies will no longer be in need of the recuperative process, for we will experience neither fatigue nor exhaustion. Our bodies will be like His glorious body (Philippians 3:21).

Huge building funds will no longer be necessary, for John says, *"I saw no temple in it,* for the Lord God, the Almighty, and the Lamb are its temple" (Revelation 21:22, italics added). We will dwell in the immmediate presence of God.

The Bible ends where it began, but *with the curse abolished.* "And there shall no longer be any curse" (Revelation 22:3). Through the cross, the curse has been removed, and replaced by eternal bliss.

There are also several positive characteristics of our heavenly home. These are not mere streets of gold and pearly gates, but things that have spiritual and eternal values.

Glory. "I desire that they also, whom Thou hast given Me, be with Me where I am, in order that they may behold My glory" (John 17:24).

"The city has no need of the sun or of the moon to shine upon it, for the glory of God has illumined it, and its lamp is the Lamb" (Revelation 21:23).

Holiness. "For thus says the high and exalted One . . . 'I dwell in a high and holy place' " (Isaiah 57:15).

"Nothing unclean, and no one who practices abomination and lying, shall ever come into it, but only those whose names are written in the Lamb's book of life" (Revelation 21:27).

Beauty. "Out of Zion, the perfection of beauty, God has shone forth" (Psalm 50:2). In heaven every aesthetic desire and aspiration will find fulfillment.

Light. "They shall not have need of the light of a lamp nor the light of the sun, because the Lord God shall illumine them" (Revelation 22:5).

Unity. In heaven the Lord's prayer in the upper room will have its complete answer. "I do not ask in behalf of these alone, but for those also who believe in Me through their word . . . that they may be one, just as We are one" (John 17:20-22). There will be a harmony and unity akin to that which exists between the members of the Godhead.

Perfection. "When the perfect comes, the partial will be done away" (1 Corinthians 13:10). In heaven we shall attain to full maturity. "When He appears we shall be like Him, because we shall see Him just as He is" (1 John 3:2).

Joy. "In Thy presence is fulness of joy, In Thy right hand there are pleasures forever" (Psalm 16:11).

Satisfaction. "I will be satisfied with Thy likeness when I awake" (Psalm 17:15). In heaven no holy desire or aspiration will remain unsatisfied.

HEAVEN'S ACTIVITIES

Few have any clear idea of the manner in which we will be occupied in heaven. Much is unrevealed in this area, but we do know that the following activities, among others, will engage us:

Worship and adoration. We will take delight in joining the twenty-four elders, representative of all redeemed humanity, who "fall down before Him who sits on the throne, and will worship Him who lives forever and ever, and will cast their crowns before the throne" (Revelation 4:10).

Music holds a prominent place in the imagery of heaven, as it did in the worship of both tabernacle and Temple and continues today in the contemporary church. There were 288 musicians employed in the Temple service (1 Chronicles 25:1-8). Both instrumental and vocal music are cited as adding to the felicity of heaven (Revelation 5:8-9). If earthly choirs and orchestras can lift us to such heights of enjoyment and praise to God, what must heaven's music be like?

Fellowship. There will be time and leisure to cultivate new friendships with saints of all ages.

Service. "For this reason, they are before the throne of God; and they serve Him day and night in His temple" (Revelation 7:15). "And His bondservants shall serve Him" (Revelation 22:3) — but in bodies that will then know no limitations. "Heaven is more than rest and beatific vision." Our Lord made it clear that in the heavenly state there will be degrees of responsibility delegated to His servants as a reward for faithfulness in service on earth. "And He said to him, . . . 'be in authority over ten cities' " (Luke 19:17).

Reunion with loved ones. If we were unable to know one another in heaven, then heaven to us would be a retrograde step. There we will know more, not less. There is no indication in Scripture that any relationship of our spiritual life will be destroyed.

> Sunset and evening star,
>   And one clear call for me!
> And may there be no moaning of the bar
>   When I put out to sea,
> But such a tide as moving seems asleep,
>   Too full for sound and foam,
> When that which drew from out the boundless deep
>   Turns again home.
>
> Twilight and evening bell,
>   And after that the dark!
> And may there be no sadness of farewell
>   When I embark.
> For though from out the bourne of time and place
>   The flood may bear me far,
> I hope to see my Pilot face to face
>   When I have crost the bar.
>
>   Alfred, Lord Tennyson

Mary in the garden and the disciples on the Emmaus road recognized the risen Christ. Peter, James, and John were introduced to Moses and Elijah. In the heavenly life conjugal relations are not the same as on earth (Luke 20:35-36), for there is no death, and therefore no need for procreation for the continuance of the human race. All will be immortal.

> Our occupation in heaven for all eternity will consist in a profound participation in the interpersonal love of the Father, the Son and the Holy Spirit. This in turn disposes us for a deeper encounter with our fellow men in heaven. Trying to enter more deeply into this perfect dialogue of love in the Trinity would be for aging man an ideal initiation and anticipation of his eternal future.[1]

The great musician Mozart, who died at 35, wrote this astonishing letter to his father on April 4, 1787:

> Since death (to be precise) is the true end and purpose of our life, I have made it my business over the past few years to get to know this true, this best friend of man so well that the thought of him not only holds no terrors for me, but even brings me great comfort and peace of mind. I thank my God that He has granted me the good fortune and opportunity to get to know death as the key to our true happiness. I never go to bed without reflecting on the thought that perhaps, as young as I am, the next day I might not be alive any more. And no man who knows me will be able to say that in social intercourse I am morose or sad. For this happiness I thank every day my Creator, and with all my heart I wish this happiness for all my fellow-men.[2]

NOTES

1. Alfons Deeken, *Growing Old* (New York: Paulist, 1972), p. 98.
2. Ibid., p. 99.

17

Whose Faith Follow

For the aging Christian, no character study in the Bible is more stimulating, encouraging, and yet challenging than that of Caleb, son of Jephunneh. At every stage of life he demonstrated the strength, beauty, and wholesomeness of a God-controlled life. When he wrote his poem, *The Oak,* Tennyson might well have had Caleb as his subject.

Live thy life
Young and old
Like yon oak,
Bright in Spring,
Living gold;

Summer — rich
Then; and then
Autumn — changed,
Soberer — hued,
Gold again

All his leaves
Fall'n at length
Look, he stands
Trunk and bough
Naked strength

Caleb was a foreigner, a stranger to the commonwealth of Israel. But he "broke his birth's invidious bar" and became "an Israelite indeed." The meaning of his name is, "all heart," and he was certainly a worthy counterpart of John Bunyan's Mr. Greatheart, for he lived up to the ideal of his name.

In early life he proved to be a man of unsinning moral and *spiritual courage.* He courageously espoused a minority cause, nor

129

did he retract or tone down his report when the stones began to fly (Numbers 14:10).

He was also a man of *undaunted faith* in a prevailing atmosphere of unbelief. When the ten spies presented their daunting and pessimistic report on prospects in the Promised Land, it was Caleb who stilled the people and injected a shot of invincible faith into the depressing atmosphere.

"We are well able to overcome it" (Numbers 13:30, KJV).

That magnificent blending of faith and courage, unfortunately, failed to elicit a positive response from the nation. But Caleb himself emerged from the encounter with flying colors.

It would be difficult to conceive a more depressing middle-life environment than that to which Israel's unbelief and failure condemned Caleb. Few have faced so hard and embittering a lot—the forty best years of his life spent wandering aimlessly in the desert. As a result of their rebellion, God had said that that whole faithless generation—Caleb and Joshua alone excepted—would die in the desert. That meant that those forty desert years were one long funeral. One by one Caleb saw his contemporaries die in that depressing situation, but once again he demonstrated his spiritual stature.

Often in middle life there develops a loss of spiritual fervor, and the spiritual life becomes insipid and anemic. The ardent love for Christ of youthful days is replaced by a dull sense of duty. The temptation to ease up on self-discipline and to accept the lowering of early ideals is all too easy to embrace, and an unconscious spiritual deterioration sets in.

Caleb, however, did not diminish in spiritual stature at that stage of life; but maintained his integrity, and emerged from the gruelling years resilient and buoyant in faith.

He had soared like an eagle in his youth. He had mastered the art of running without growing weary in middle age. But would he now be able to walk and not faint in his old age? It was in his advanced years that he achieved his greatest victory.

Caleb demonstrated the possibility of turning what is often viewed as the tragedy of old age into a glorious triumph. At the age of eighty-five, he displayed ageless and adventurous youthfulness of spirit. The hero of forty years of age is no less a hero when he reaches eighty-five years. For him, old age was not senility, but aggression and achievement. When most of his younger contemporaries were thinking only of the serenity of retirement and leisure, he was planning new and demanding adventure that would have daunted a much younger man. He had the strength and virility of youth still.

True, he had the great advantage of vigorous good health. "I am still as strong today as I was in the day Moses sent me; as my strength was then, so my strength is now, for war and for going out and coming in" (Joshua 14:11). That boon is not granted to the majority of aging people, but Caleb's robust health evidenced his life of self-discipline.

The delay in God's fulfillment of the promise made to Caleb did not quench his confidence, or dampen his ardor. His was not a triumph of physical strength, although that was involved. It was essentially the victory of an optimistic and dauntless spirit. Even in old age he remained spiritually adacious. He was ambitious to rout the enemies of God and bring their territory under His dominion.

ADVENTUROUS IN OLD AGE

Joshua was dividing the land among the people of the nation (Joshua 14:6-15). When it came to Caleb's allotment, the request he made of Joshua revealed the calibre of the man:

"Now then, *give me this hill country* [mountain, KJV] about which the Lord spoke on that day, for you heard on that day that the Anakim were there, with great fortified cities; perhaps the Lord will be with me, and I shall drive them out as the Lord has spoken" (Joshua 14:12, italics added).

No fertile river flat for Caleb! He chose the most difficult assignment in the whole nation—the rugged mountain that housed the three invincible giants. Such was his ambitious request, and he eagerly accepted the challenge it offered, counting on his God to give him victory over the enemies of his people.

Caleb was the only one of whom it is recorded that he wholly subdued the territory allotted to him, and totally evicted the enemy. So *his last years were his best,* the crown and culmination of all that had gone before.

What an inspiring example for us elderly folk to seek to emulate in our measure! We may lack his physique, but it should be borne in mind that his was the victory of his spirit and of his faith in God. A similar triumph over our adverse circumstances and a like achievement for the kingdom of God is open to us.

Caleb was satisfied with nothing less than God's best — and he obtained it. Are we aging people losing our spirit of aggression? Do we shrink from the rigors of spiritual battle? Let us remove our slippers, don our mountaineering boots, and ask God to give us some menacing mountain to conquer in our old age.

> Make me to be Thy happy mountaineer,
>   O God most high;
> My climbing soul would welcome the austere:
>   Lord, crucify
> On rock or scree, ice-cliff or field of snow,
> The softness that would sink to things below.
>   Amy Wilson Carmichael

Index of Persons

Index of Scripture

Moody Press, a ministry of the Moody Bible Institute, is designed for education, evangelization, and edification. If we may assist you in knowing more about Christ and the Christian life, please write us without obligation: Moody Press, c/o MLM, Chicago, Illinois 60610.

76779